Praise for Authentic Alignment:

"Dr. Asha Prasad has put together a stroi
to reclaim their personal power and to h
promised, Asha delivers a sure, sound, ε
transformation. Thank you, Dr. Asha, for this contribution to humanity."

-**Dr. Sue Morter**, founder of the Morter Institute for BioEnergetics
and Healing and developer of *The Energy Codes:
Principles and Practices for Embodying Your Most Full Potential*

"Take control of your health for a better life! I am so grateful to have found
a book that finally gives me some straight answers about understanding
what it means to be in control when it comes to my own health. *Authentic
Alignment* has opened my eyes in so many ways. It has made me realize
that I am guilty, like so many of us, of taking my own health for granted.
I've come to realize that is not a strategy but an excuse — and not a good
one. So much of what we do in life isn't possible if we aren't feeling optimal,
and yet most of us haven't a clue how to take control of our health and well-
being. This book certainly changes that perspective and will undoubtedly
help you as much as it has helped me to find a healthy balance and lead a
more rewarding and fulfilling life."

-**Steve Harper**, author of *The Ripple Effect:
Maximizing the Power of Relationships for Your Life and Business*

"What an inspiring, uplifting book! You are in for a treat as you fly through
the pages allowing Dr. Asha Prasad to animate and motivate you, provoke
and enliven your mind, and entice your inner wisdom and deepest knowing to willingly reveal itself, sparking realizations that have the potential to
exhilarate your spirit and infuse your life with new-found enthusiasm. Go
on this journey through the pages with her to recapture that fully switched-

on vibrant feeling from your youth, when you absolutely knew what felt intrinsically right for you. I dare you to!

"Asha shares her knowledge, wisdom and insights with you in this book because she truly cares about making a positive difference in your life and in the world. She encourages you to stand tall and be the best you that she absolutely knows is waiting to really reveal itself to the world. Asha's wisdom, passion, integrity and inspiring presence will help one person, one group, one nation, one continent, one world, one Universe at a time until we discover that the seeds she has sown here have impacted and created the harmonious world that we all wish for. By reading this book and putting into practice the philosophies she has shared with us, you too play a huge integral part in creating that enlightened, peaceful, respectful world we all desire.

"I know that all of you who choose to journey with her, through her book, her online teachings and her one-to-one or group sessions will emerge transformed, shining brighter and feeling happier with life itself. I wish you all a very enjoyable journey!"

-**Jo Helesfay-Evans**, founder of the Illumination System Technique and proprietor of Inner Light Holistics

AUTHENTIC
ALIGNMENT

AUTHENTIC ALIGNMENT

HOW ANCIENT WISDOM AND MODERN SCIENCE CAN REVITALIZE YOUR HEALTH, HAPPINESS AND POTENTIAL

Dr. Asha M. Prasad

A-NU
VISION

ISBN: 97809964194-2-0

Published by A-NU Vision

www. theprasadmethod.com

"The love of a family is life's greatest blessing."

-Unknown

This book is dedicated to my parents and sister.
Thank you for your ever-present encouragement, love and support.
Without it, none of this would be possible.

Table of Contents

Preface

"Life isn't about finding yourself. Life is about creating yourself."

-George Bernard Shaw

Peple write books for all sorts of reasons: ego, money, wish fulfillment, the need to share a story. There's nothing wrong with any of
those reasons, but I wrote this one for a different reason altogether:
confirmation.

You see, this book is a confirmation of a re-imagining of my life that
began just a few years ago, a radical transformation in how I perceived my
own health and happiness and, gradually, the dawning awareness that my
personal journey might offer some insight and encouragement to others
facing similar challenges.

At the time, I was deeply enmeshed in the rat race. To all outward appearances, I was personally and professionally successful. The future seemed
bright, the present a blur of activity. More than once, friends and colleagues
said something to the effect of "Asha, you've got it all together."

The truth, however, was far different. I was a mess, my health deterio-
rating alarmingly. I was deeply unhappy and disenchanted with my life.
And I finally realized that I needed to make some changes.

Big changes. Drastic changes.

I looked beyond the blood work and physical symptoms to come to
grips with the underlying causes of my dysfunction. I began researching
people who lived authentically, who marched to the beat of their own
drummer, who had the fortitude to listen to the voice of their inner self
instead of the insistent chorus of those around them, who excelled in aligning their personal and professional goals. I sought out mentors who faced
the world on their terms instead of its terms, soaking in their wisdom and

perspective. I completed coursework to give myself the knowledge and the ability to embrace what I became convinced was the right course of action for me.

I was fortunate to have the encouragement and support of many of my family and friends during this time, although there were others who openly questioned whether I could sustain the changes I was making and a few who thought I'd gone off the deep end. It was definitely a time of testing.

But then something wonderful happened: I got better, and not just physically. My entire being — physical, mental, emotional and spiritual — became healthier and happier. I felt, for the first time, like the different facets of my life were in sync, that I was doing what I was meant to do the way I was meant to do it. I called this new lifestyle an "authentic alignment."

My change in perspective also changed how I related to my patients, many of whom I noticed were struggling with the same challenges that I had been. I shared with them the same techniques and modalities I was using in my own life . . . and I witnessed the same positive transformations in theirs. And the more I saw, the greater the urgency I felt to share with an even wider audience the lessons I had learned: you have the power within you to create the life you want, the life you deserve.

In the pages that follow, I hope I can provide you with some tools and strategies for creating a more authentically aligned life for yourself. I'm confident that if you do, the results will be far richer and more satisfying than you could have ever envisioned.

In writing this book, I am especially indebted to the insights and contributions of a number of trailblazers in the fields of alternative medicine, spirituality, and mental health, especially the mentors and teachers who have shared their wisdom with me over the years. You have been a generous, inspirational, and constant catalyst for others to be their true selves, including me. I am especially grateful to Jo Helesfay-Evans and Dominique Baudoux for their friendship, support, and teaching. Dr. Sue Morter, you have been an inspiration in so many ways, as well as a valued mentor and guide in my personal and professional journey.

There are many others who have played a major role in my life, both personally and professionally — too many, unfortunately, to list individually here. But please know that I cherish and appreciate all that you have done to support and encourage me in all my endeavors.

I would be remiss if I didn't single a few of you out by name, though. First and foremost, a big "thank you" to Marc Schwarz for saying yes to joining me on this journey. Our mutual dear friend Steve Harper reconnected us over a year ago and it has been a beautiful harmonious working relationship. You really have a great talent and ability for knowing exactly what is needed. I am grateful for your expertise and the time that you took to work on this project. You are greatly appreciated, and I look forward to collaborating on future projects as well.

Steve Harper, you are an inspiration. Now that we are separated by the Atlantic Ocean we don't have the opportunity to see each other face-to-face as much as we used to, but your encouragement in our phone conversations and email exchanges helped revitalize my dream of writing a book. You have always shown true support and care, and I'm proud to not only know you, but to count you as a friend. Your input on my journey has been truly invaluable. Thank you.

To my dear friends and family, your support and encouragement have been vital not only to this project, but to the person I have become and am still becoming.

I am deeply grateful for you all, and I look forward to a great deal more fun and adventure with you on this shared journey of life. Thank you for everything.

Asha M. Prasad
April, 2016

Introduction

"No matter how much we try to run away from this thirst for the answer to life, for the meaning of life, the intensity only gets stronger and stronger. We cannot escape these spiritual hungers."

-Ravi Zacharias

At the end of the 1983 Monty Python film *The Meaning of Life*, a drag-clad Michael Palin opens an envelope and casually reads the answer to the question that has provided the narrative framework for the movie: "Try and be nice to people, avoid eating fat, read a good book every now and then, get some walking in, and try and live together in peace and harmony with people of all creeds and nations."

It's an intentionally anticlimactic moment, a conscious counterpoint to the existential angst of early 80s Britain. Palin's character bitterly acknowledges that something more graphic or controversial would probably be more successful in attracting audiences. Cut to the closing credits.

There's no shortage of pontificating on the nature of the meaning of life, and certainly no lack of films, television shows, paintings, books, poems, speeches, sermons and social media memes offering perspectives on how to maximize our time on this planet. "What's the meaning of life?" is in all probability the single most-asked question in the entire history of the human race.

Western societies have generally equated purpose and fulfillment with material accomplishment, which has led to unparalleled economic achievement, scientific discovery and technological development . . . as well as millions of prescriptions for anti-anxiety medications, 80-hour work weeks and deep-rooted interpersonal dysfunction. For many of us, it's almost as though the more we achieve, the less we receive — at least at the level that matters most.

It's a phenomenon that affects even those who have accomplished feats unknown to all but a handful of humans. Astronaut Alan Bean was the fourth man to walk on the moon, a member of as select a fraternity as you could imagine. But just hours after Apollo 12 lifted off from the lunar surface, Bean recalls feeling a profound sense of anti-climax. "It's kind of like the song," he confided in his two crewmates on the journey home. "Is that all there is?"

Is that all there is? The question is a haunting one. For too many of us, life is an endless cycle of waking up, going to work, coming home, eating (too much) and sleeping (not enough). And at some point, we all hit the metaphorical wall: is this all there is? Is this my life? What happened? How did all those hopes of a happy, fulfilled life become little more than a hope that we can make next month's mortgage payment? When did dreams give way to fears: financial fears, relationship fears, health fears?

If you've ever woken up dreading another day at the rat race, this book is for you. If you've ever felt disconnected from your life, this book is for you. If you've ever ignored your body's warning signs because you "didn't have time to be sick," this book is for you. If you've ever looked in the mirror and wondered, like Alan Bean, if this is all there is, this book is for you. If you've ever wanted a deeper, more meaningful, more fulfilling life, then this book is definitely for you.

You have a choice. You can suppress, you can self-medicate, you can attempt to distract yourself. Or you can begin to reframe the nature of your own personal reality. You can change your life. You can change the destination of your life's journey. You can change your future . . . starting now.

Of course, change isn't easy. Embracing the unknown never is. It's no accident that the most famous soliloquy in the English language — the "to be or not to be" speech from Shakespeare's Hamlet — deals not just with the existential question of the meaning of life, but also with our self-imposed paralysis to take charge of our own destinies. "Thus doth conscience make cowards of us all," laments Hamlet. My (very loose) translation: we spend so much time dwelling on the problems, real and imagined, that we never get around to actually implementing solutions.

Alan Bean wrestled with the feelings awakened by his trip to the moon and back and eventually decided to leave NASA . . . in order to become a full-time artist. Needless to say, within the fighter jock atmosphere of the astronaut corps, this was a radical and little understood lifestyle change. Nevertheless, he persevered, eventually refining his technique into a mixture of painting and sculpture — even incorporating small pieces of various Apollo spacecraft and a sprinkling of moon dust. Today his paintings sell for tens of thousands, even hundreds of thousands, of dollars. More importantly, Bean has found a fulfillment in his art that not even his time on the lunar surface could provide.

I'm going to challenge you to take a similar leap of faith. Within these pages, you will find both practical strategies and foundational theory to make profound and lasting emotional, mental, spiritual and physical changes in your life. We'll begin by wrestling with various perspectives, both contemporary and traditional, and the meaning of health. Then, in Chapters Three and Four, we'll examine the interconnectedness of the various aspects of health: physical, mental, emotional, and spiritual. In Chapter Five, you'll have the chance to self-assess your current level of authentically aligned health to identify areas of strength and opportunities for growth.

Beginning in Chapter Six, our focus turns to practical and sustainable tools for addressing each of the four areas of aligned health: Each chapter offers a variety of exercises for beginners, as well as intermediate and advanced practitioners. My hope is that you will not only find what works best for your situation, but that you will also challenge yourself as your level of health and skill improves.

The book concludes with some final thoughts and recommendations from me, as well as a list of resources for further study or reading. *Authentic Alignment* is, after all, intended as the beginning of a new and more satisfying life for you, not its culmination.

I only ask that you read the pages that follow with an open mind and heart. Embrace the concepts and tools that speak most powerfully to you;

let the rest fall away or reference it for a future experience. Give yourself permission to live out the words of author Anaïs Nin: "There is not one big cosmic meaning for all; there is only the meaning we each give to our life, an individual meaning, an individual plot, like an individual novel, a book for each person."

Let's go finish writing *your* book!

Chapter One
What is Health?

"From so simple a beginning, endless forms most beautiful and most wonderful have been, and are being evolved."

-*Charles Darwin*, The Origin of Species

In the beginning, there was you. Of course, *you* weren't the person you see in the mirror or in your Facebook selfies — not yet, anyway. Instead, you were a tiny glob of cells less than a hundredth of an inch across. The scientific term for this structure is a blastocyst, which seems frustratingly impersonal and unromantic given the series of miracles unfolding over the next three-quarters of a year. As Barry Werth writes in *From Conception to Birth*:

> Imagine yourself as the world's tallest skyscraper, built in 9 months and germinating from a single brick. As that "seed" brick divides, it gives rise to every other type of material needed to construct and operate the finished tower — a million tons of steel, concrete, mortar, insulation, tile, wood, granite, solvents, carpet, cable, pipe, and glass as well as all furniture, phone systems, heating and cooling units, plumbing, electrical wiring, artwork, and computer networks, including software. The brick and its daughter bricks also know exactly how much of each to make, where to send them, and when and how to piece it all together. Now imagine further that when the building is done it has the capacity to love, hate, converse, do calculus, compose symphonies, and have rapturous physical

relations with other towers, a prime result of which is to create new buildings even more elaborate than itself.

Perhaps even more amazingly, this massive biological building project happens automatically, with neither the developing embryo nor the expectant mother consciously guiding the process or aware of the specifics. Within just a few weeks of your conception, the blastocyst (still less than a tenth of an inch across) curls into the shape of a tiny comma. A groove running along the length of the back emerges, then closes into a tube: the origin of your spinal column. Long, stringy cells emerge from the tube and connect to a bulge at the top of the comma: the beginnings of your brain and nervous system. Two narrow slits form: your eyes. Another tube of cells forms and twists into an S-shaped loop near the center of the embryo; possessing the ability to spontaneously contract and expand, within three weeks this new structure is sending oxygen- and nutrient-rich cells to every part of the tiny organism. Your heart has begun beating.

Like some sort of sci-fi origami, the embryo's tissues fold and refold themselves at breakneck speed; neurons proliferate at the rate of 100,000 per hour. Bulges on the sides become more recognizable as emerging limbs. Two months after conception, a face is dimly but clearly visible. Finger "rays" and nipples form, although the being that is "you" is still about the size of raisin.

By the end of the first trimester, your body's blueprint is complete and you begin to resemble a mature human being. The head becomes more rounded. Eyelids and articulated outer ears can be seen. Muscles respond to increasing signals from the brain, causing you to kick, bend your arms, curl your toes and make a fist. You are also opening your mouth, squinting your eyes (although they remain shut, still several months away from providing you with your first sights), pursing your lips. Your liver, kidneys, lungs and digestive systems are all evident, although obviously the fetus — no longer just an embryo — still has a long way to go before it can survive outside the womb.

During the second trimester you begin packing on the weight, quadrupling it in just the fourth month alone. Your gender, genetically determined at the outset but indistinguishable by even microscopic visible means until several weeks later, now can be seen even by most laypeople during a routine ultrasound. On the tips of your fingers and toes, distinctive whorls and ridges appear: your fingerprints, each individual's set as unique as a snowflake. Soon you begin to turn and kick with enough force to alert your mother and produce squeals of delight from family and friends who feel your movements through her abdominal wall. The 300 bones you will be born with (some of which will later fuse together, giving you an adult total of 206) are hardening, and the 33 rings, 150 joints and 1,000 ligaments that make up your spine have begun to form. Your eyes flutter and open, and as your nostrils unseal you begin making breathing movements.

As your body prepares for birth, more subtle but infinitely profound changes are occurring. Grooves and furrows appear on the outer surface of your cerebral cortex, what will become the centers for sight, smell, hearing, motor control and speech. Your bone marrow begins producing red blood cells. On your head, hair begins to grow. Fingernails and toenails may have grown long enough for you to give yourself scratches in utero. Your weight is 1,000 times what it was as an embryo — usually six to eight pounds and 19 to 20 inches long. No longer a tiny heap of soap-bubble cells, you are a completely functional and viable human being, albeit one who will still require years of care-taking before you become completely self-sufficient.

Life as we know it

According to the Population Reference Bureau, between 350,000 and 400,000 people are born every day worldwide. Looked at another way, that means that each day sees the successful completion of nearly half a million versions of the most sophisticated and ingenious building project the human race has ever been associated with. In fact, nothing else comes close — not the Manhattan skyline or the International Space Station or even Britney Spears's Vegas set. In the 40 weeks between conception to birth, your body has literally engineered itself from a microscopic handful of cells, using as its blueprint the genetic code of both your parents, seamlessly combined into a pattern at once universal and completely individual. You are, by your very existence, a miraculous creation of the first order.

So what the heck happened?

Flash forward a few decades, and — for most of us, anyway — that miraculous creation looks a little ragged around the edges. According to an Institute of Medicine study, approximately 100 million Americans deal with chronic neck or back pain. One in three have chronic knee pain. Nor is the pain limited to the physical realm. A study by Medco Health Solutions found that more than one in five Americans now takes at least one drug to treat a psychological disorder, ranging from antidepressants like Prozac to anti-anxiety drugs like Xanax. And that number is increasing alarmingly, up 22% from 2001.

If it were all the result of injury or disease or old age, it might be understandable. But it's not. In fact, the number of children under 10 taking antipsychotic drugs has increased by 100% since 2001, according to the same Medco study, and there's been a 40% increase in the number of girls prescribed ADHD medicines. The frightening reality is that the biological perfection (or pretty darn close, in most cases) that we know at birth is being undermined at younger and younger ages, resulting in an ever-expanding litany of physical, emotional, spiritual and mental maladies.

And while life expectancy is significantly higher in First World nations than in the developing world (when was the last time we had a cholera epidemic, after all?) longer lives don't necessarily mean *healthier* lives. Believe it or not, affluence may actually have some profoundly negative implications for our health. A recent Arizona State University study found that children from wealthy families were more likely to develop mental health problems than children from poorer households. The researchers discovered that children whose parents earned more than $160,000 a year were twice as likely to experience clinical depression and anxiety. They also demonstrated significantly increased levels of neurosis that lead to drug abuse, criminal behavior and eating disorders. Why? The pressure to succeed, says ASU psychologist Suniya Luthar: "The evidence suggests that the privileged young are much more vulnerable than in previous generations. The evidence points to one cause: the pressure for high octane achievement. The children of affluent parents expect to excel at school and in extracurricular activities, and also in their social lives. They feel a relentless sense of pressure."

That "relentless pressure" has physical as well as mental and emotional consequences, for adults as well as children. A 2013 Tel Aviv University study published in the journal *Psychosomatic Medicine* found a link between job burnout and coronary heart disease, obesity, insomnia and anxiety. The researchers found that the top 20% of those suffering from work stress and burnout increased their risk of coronary disease by almost 80%. Another study conducted by scientists at Helmholtz Zentrum München, the German Research Center for Environmental Health, studied biological markers in the blood associated with stress. They found that those markers triggered an escalated inflammatory response from the body that resulted in a much higher risk of heart problems. Otherwise "healthy" workers exposed to work stress had higher concentrations of CRP (C-reactive protein) and, as a result, "faced twice the risk of cardiovascular disease."

Playing the blame game

So who gets the blame for this sorry state of affairs? How about our parents? It's their genes, after all, that give us our own unique "operating systems." Clearly that programming — for some of us, anyway — is a little glitchy, resulting in hereditary predispositions towards heart disease, cancer, arthritis, mental illness, diabetes . . . you name it. It's genetic determinism, and it's inescapable.

Or is it? Dr. Bruce Lipton is a pioneer in the field of epigenetics, which challenges the traditional notion that our genetic future is fixed. Back in 1967, Lipton was working with cloned stem cells, each genetically indistinguishable from its parent cell. In a petri dish, he observed as each cell divided every 10 hours or so. After a couple of weeks, he had thousands of identical cells.

That's when Lipton did something interesting. He divided the cells into three petri dishes. In each, he changed the culture medium slightly to produce three different — but not radically different — environments. What he observed was astounding. Instead of continuing to divide into identical cells, in the first petri dish the cells began to form into bone cells. In the second, they formed muscle cells. And in the third, they formed fat cells.

What had caused this radical differentiation? It had to be the different culture mediums. As Lipton remembers, "When the experiments started, all of the cells were genetically identical, and yet, they had different fates, so the obvious question is 'What controlled the fate of the cell?' The answer was, the only thing that was different was the environment. When I put all this together, of course, it didn't really jive with what I was teaching because I'm telling all the students in medical school, 'Yes, genes control the traits of the cell.' Yet clearly, the experiments revealed that genes are very important but it was the environment (that was key)."

In a 2010 interview with John Petrozzi, Lipton explained the ramifications of that discovery:

> After 30 years of research, it really came down to understanding the nature, a very simple truth, that in a petri dish, I changed the culture environment and I changed the fate of the cells.
>
> A human body really by definition – this is funny if you think about it – a human body is a skin-covered petri dish. It has 50 trillion cells living in it. So underneath your skin are 50 trillion cells in this giant petri dish. The culture medium for the cells is called "the blood." If you change the chemistry of the blood, it's the same as changing the culture medium in a plastic petri dish. So, the fate of the cells in my body is directly related to the culture medium: the blood and its chemistry.

Then, you find out, oh my goodness, the brain is like a chemist. The brain secretes the chemistry into the blood that changes the fate of the cells. But the brain doesn't do this automatically. It does it in connection with our mind, our beliefs, and our perceptions.

So if you're afraid, for example, you're releasing stress hormones into the culture medium (the blood) and that changes the fate of the cells as they get into protection. Or if you're living in love, you're releasing things like serotonin and dopamine chemistry into the blood. Those chemicals promote growth and harmony. So it's just as you switch from love to fear, you change the chemistry of your blood, and the blood chemistry controls the fate of your cells. So, your mind is controlling the genetics of your cells.

This is actually the foundation of a new science called "epigenetics." What we were teaching in school was genetics, which says, "Hey, genes control your life. You didn't pick the genes. You can't change the genes. You become a victim of your heredity."

The new science reveals that by changing your mind, you change the chemistry of the environment, and the cells respond by changing their genetics. This is called "epigenetics." Epi means "above." So, when you say "epigenetic control," literally, you're just saying, "control above the genes." Now, we know that as we perceive the world, we change our genetics.

We (used to) say, "Oh, these are your genes and that's for the rest of your life." Now, we find on a day-by-day basis that how you respond to life changes your genetics dynamically. So, if you change your perceptions and beliefs, you change your biology.

"I" vs "we"

Thanks to epigenetics, we now have a much fuller picture of why we so often become unhealthy, especially in those cases where there isn't an obvious physical cause like a pathogen. And it starts at birth.

In the womb, we are the beneficiary of a closed, self-regulating system. It may appear at times chaotic, but in fact it is highly structured and it has only one goal: the development and protection of the fetus. Once we enter the world, however, we become part of a community of individuals, a community that is rarely self-aware about how its actions impact every facet of the developing individual.

In the years that follow, our internal biological "operating system" is to some extent over-written by these external forces. Our parents, grandparents, siblings, teachers and friends impart to us their likes and dislikes, their preferences and prejudices, their virtues and peccadilloes. Our self-image is not only reflected in their behavior towards us, it's shaped by it. Without even realizing it, we adapt to win the acceptance of those we depend on for both physical and emotional sustenance.

So when we hear statements like "Stop acting like a girl!" or "Tough it out!" we internalize their message, which can unconsciously create conflict with our own individualized code. That conflict produces stress, and stress — as has been well documented — leads inexorably to poor health.

Please don't misunderstand: I'm not advocating that we all become hermits. In fact, there are also some well-documented benefits to being part of a community. Multiple studies have shown that married individuals, on average, outlive their single counterparts. Seniors active in their community also live longer and, again on average, enjoy fewer health problems than more withdrawn peers. We are social animals, and the benefits of regular, purposeful interaction seem to outweigh the drawbacks.

A great example of the positive power of community is the story of Pierre Dulaine, a world-renowned ballroom dancer who started an arts-in-education program called Dancing Classrooms in 1994. Its mission is to build social awareness, confidence and self-esteem in elementary school students, particularly those identified as being "at risk" of dropping out because they come from low socioeconomic families. According to Dancing Classrooms' website, "Through ballroom dance, students break down social barriers, learn about honor and respect, improve self confidence, communicate and cooperate, and accept others even if they are different."

The Dancing Classrooms approach has proven consistently successful because of how ballroom dancing is taught: the so-called Dulaine Method. The foundation of the Dulaine Method is the notion of respect, both for others as well as for one's self. That in turn creates a safe environment filled with positive reinforcement — a critical component in getting self-conscious preteens to buy in to the process. "The Dulaine Method is so effective because it allows for a very natural learning process to occur," says Carmen Barken, an LA-based instructor for Dancing Classrooms. "It is built on fun, compassion, control and safety — emotional as well as physical."

Beginning in just two New York City schools, the Dancing Classrooms movement has now spread to over two dozen cities worldwide. In an era in which high stakes standardized testing has prompted school districts across the country to cut arts programs in favor of more classroom "seat time," Dulaine's approach has been credited with reducing incidents of bullying, chronic absenteeism and dropouts, and increasing student focus, self-esteem and academic achievement. It's a great example of how the power of a focused community can be used to improve the individuals who belong to it, who in turn benefit the community as a whole: a feedback loop of positivity.

That said, we shouldn't be blind to those potential drawbacks of community, either. Just within the past few years, there has been a re-definition of adolescent bullying to include indirect and non-physical aspects, which some studies suggest are just as harmful as direct, physical bullying. In fact, although physical bullying seems to decrease as students age, verbal and psychological abuse appears to remain constant. Moreover, this "indirect" bullying seems to defy school size, racial composition, and school setting (rural, suburban, or urban). The rise of social media has even led to so-called "cyber bullying," whose effects can be just as devastating.

Several studies have confirmed that this constant stream of negativity can result in both psychological and physical distress, with victims of in-direct bullying becoming physically ill. And it's not just teenagers who are susceptible to the relentless drumbeat of peer pressure; it affects us at every age and every season of life. And that's a problem. When our sense of self is so rooted in an external locus, it can cause us to lose faith in our own body's innate wisdom and create the seeds of poor health.

Re-thinking health

Because of emerging disciplines like epigenetics, we are more aware than ever of the powerful connection between our physical and psychological well-being. That realization has prompted a gradual re-assessment of the concept of health itself, which has proven surprisingly elusive. In the next chapter, we'll engage in a little bit of time travel to examine how our ances-tors viewed health, and how various historic medical traditions have im-pacted, with both positive and negative effects, the evolution of our own health care industry.

We'll also begin to discover how some ancient wisdom is now being validated by 21st-century science, with some amazing implications for you and your quest for a healthier, happier, more authentically aligned life. It's an exciting time to be alive!

Chapter Two

A Brief History of Health

"There is deep wisdom within our very flesh,
if we can only come to our senses and feel it."

-Elizabeth A. Behnke

It's not an exaggeration to say that Americans are obsessed by — and conflicted about — their health. On the one hand, we spend over $60 billion annually just on taking off excess pounds: gym memberships, diet foods, weight-loss programs.[1] On the other hand, the latest annual survey of the 34 member countries of the Organization for Economic Cooperation and Development (OECD) shows that many Americans are losing the battle of the bulge. Almost 37% of American adults are classified as "obese," compared to 18% of Canadians, 15% of Germans, and 11% of Dutch. The Swiss are the sveltest among the European OECD member states, coming in at just over 8%. That's still a long way from the skinniest nation on the list, Japan, where only 4% of the adult population is classified as obese.

Of course, that $60 billion in weight loss spending pales in comparison to the total amount that Americans spend annually on healthcare, estimated by the Deloitte Center for Health Solutions to be as high as $3.8 *trillion* and rising. Included in that figure is $259 billion in prescription drugs. Writing in *The Atlantic*, Victor Fuchs points out that:

> The U.S. far outspends its peer nations when it comes
> to healthcare costs per capita. This year the United States

---

[1] *According to a 2013 report by Marketdata Enterprises, a market research firm that specializes in tracking niche industries.*

will spend almost 18 percent of the gross domestic product (GDP) on healthcare — six percentage points more than the Netherlands, the next highest spender. Because the U.S. GDP in 2014 will be approximately 17 trillion dollars, those six percentage points over the Netherlands amount to one trillion dollars in additional spending. The burden to the average household through lost wages, insurance premiums, taxes, out-of-pocket care, and other costs will be more than $8,000.

With all that we spend on our health, surely we're getting our money's worth, right? Uh, not so fast. According to a report from the U.S. National Research Council's Institute of Medicine, "On nearly all indicators of mortality, survival, and life expectancy, the United States ranks at or near the bottom among high-income countries." In other words, we're spending more and getting less. Yikes!

Multiple meanings

To explain this apparent contradiction between how much we annually spend on healthcare and how healthy (or unhealthy) we truly are, perhaps it's illuminating to take a step back and think about what it means to be "healthy." Read the following sentences and reflect on the multiple shades of meaning we've assigned this innocuous but omnipresent word:

- "I'm really worried about how healthy it is for my husband to be working out in the hot summer sun all day without a break."

- "You know what they say: if you don't have your health, you don't have anything."

- "I know that it's not healthy to keep working these 90-hour weeks, but what can I do?"

- "Job creation is one sign of a healthy economy."

- "My nephew sure has a healthy appetite!"

- "Given how much crime has increased in our neighborhood over the past five years, I'm not sure how healthy it is to keep living here."

- "This year, we've made a family commitment to eat healthy."

Depending on the context in the sentences above, "healthy" implies the absence of injury or illness, mental well-being, robustness, abundance, physical safety, or selectivity. That's pretty impressive range of meaning for just seven letters! In etymological terms, the English word "health" comes from the Old English word *hale*, meaning "wholeness, being whole, sound or well." *Hale* comes from the Proto-Indo-European root *kailo*, which means "whole, uninjured, of good omen."

Western medical science, however, has been until relatively recently much more circumspect in how it defines health, generally using some variation of "the absence of any disease or impairment." In 1948, the World Health Organization expanded that limited definition of health in its founding constitution: "Health is a state of complete physical, mental and social well-being and not merely the absence of disease or infirmity."

Other practitioners define health as a state that allows the individual to adequately cope with all demands of daily life (implying also the absence of disease and impairment). A third definition describes health is a state of balance, an equilibrium that individuals establish *within* themselves as well as *between* themselves and their social and physical environments.

For the most part, though, it's still that first definition that holds sway: *the absence of any disease or impairment.* And within that mindset lies both the power and the limitations of Western medicine. To understand how that mindset developed, let's take a look at the three ancient cultures that most influenced the development of Western medical thought: the Mesopotamians, the Egyptians, and the Greco-Romans.

Surgeons and sorcerers

Digging into the roots of Western medicine requires literal digging . . . into the library of Ashurbanipal, the last great king of Assyria. When the Assyrian capital, Nineveh — near the modern Iraqi city of Mosul — was destroyed in 612 B.C., the royal palace and other important buildings were torn down and buried by the conquerors, a confederation of former vassals led by the Medes and Babylonians. (The Assyrians were not exactly popular rulers, it must be admitted.) Nineveh was rediscovered by Europeans only in the mid-1800s. In 1853, a young British adventurer named Sir Austen Henry Layard was exploring the ruins when he stumbled across a ditch filled with clay tablets: the contents of Ashurbanipal's famous library.

Once tallied, the haul was over 22,000 tablets covered with short, wedge-shaped lines — cuneiform, the writing of the Mesopotamian world. And since Ashurbanipal's scribes habitually copied and recopied ancient tablets, many of the texts discovered are actually far older than his reign — perhaps as much as a thousand years older. Layard had discovered one of the world's great treasure troves of knowledge.

Out of the 22,000 tablets recovered, 660 were of a medical nature. Archaeologists have grouped those with similar entries into "treatises," the largest of which (about 3,000 entries on 40 tablets) has been dubbed the "Treatise of Medical Diagnoses and Prognoses." It's basically a head-to-toe list of diseases and conditions designed to assist the medical practitioner in evaluating a patient. Despite the scientific-sounding title, though — and the fact that the treatise does accurately describe the symptoms of conditions like jaundice — the fact is that ancient Mesopotamian medicine was usually a choice between primitive first aid implemented by an *asu*, or "physician," and outright magic, practiced by an *ashipu*, or "sorcerer."

The approaches were distinct but often complementary. Here's how an *ashipu* might approach an injury: "If a man has a blow on the cheek, practical prescription for this: Bray [a plant] in water from the well of Marduk, collect therein dust from four crossroads . . . Seven and seven times cleanse his mouth."

And here's how an *asu* might deal with the same issue: "If a man is sick with a blow on the cheek: pound together fir-turpentine, pine-turpentine, tamarisk, daisy, flour of Inninnu. Strain; mix in milk and beer in a small copper pan; spread on skin, bind on him, and he shall recover."

By the time of King Ashurbanipal a third option had emerged: surgery. The law recognized three paths to health: "the art of healing with drugs," "the prescriptions of the sorcerers," and "the way of operating with the brass knife." Few treatises deal with the latter course of treatment, but the famous Code of Hammurabi actually did mention it:

> *215. If a physician performed a major operation on a seignior with a bronze lancet and has saved the seignior's life . . . he shall receive ten shekels of silver.*

> *216. If it was a member of the commonality, he shall receive five shekels.*

> *217. If it was a seignior's slave, the owner of the slave shall give two shekels of silver to the physician.*

> *218. If a physician performed a major operation on a seignior with a bronze lancet and has caused the seignior's death . . . they shall cut off his hand.*

In ancient Mesopotamia, surgery was definitely a high-risk, high-reward proposition . . . for both patient and physician. Provided that he did not make an actual incision, however, it appears that the practitioner could not be held liable for a negative outcome. Not illogically, it appears that most *asu* usually preferred a pharmacological course of treatment: creating a unique poultice, or *bultu*, by collecting a mixture of herbs and other ingredients (including such exotic items as lizard dung), then pounding them together, then cooking and straining the resulting mushy paste. The *bultu* could be swallowed, applied topically, administered as an enema, or even inhaled.

Primitive though Mesopotamian medicine might have been, it established one of the key principles of Western medicine, namely that disease is external. It could be caused by an evil spirit, a god, a ghost, cold, dust, even a bad smell. The remedy was designed to excise the outside agent and/or create a protective barrier against it.

Of course, instead of using aspirin and antibiotics, the originators of Western medicine used ground-up turtle shells and ammonium salt. Still, it's the thought that counts.

Medicine in the shadow of the pyramids

A thousand miles away from Nineveh, another medical culture was taking shape: the Egyptians. The earliest mention of an Egyptian physician dates back to around 2600 B.C.; a narrow stone slab called a stela offers a hieroglyphic profile of Hesy-Ra, Chief of Dentists and Physicians to the rulers of the Third Dynasty. We don't know much about his practice, but the images on the stela depict Hesy-Ra as a learned man.

The earliest Egyptian medical text is a battered papyrus scroll created around 1900 B.C. We've discovered a half dozen others, spaced out over the succeeding 800 years. Taken as a whole, there are roughly 1200 short paragraphs that provide short descriptions of diseases, curative spells, or prescriptions. The similarities to Mesopotamian methods are immediately apparent.

Unlike their Mesopotamian counterparts, however, surgery seems to have been much less common. Evidence of suturing can be seen in mummies dating back to around 1100 B.C., although it's clear that those stitches were made post mortem by embalmers, not physicians. We also know that the Egyptians used a variety of adhesive strips, mainly gum from acacia trees, to bind up wounds.

The Egyptians are also notable in recognizing the presence of infection — they divided injuries into "sick wounds" and "not sick wounds." Here's how an Egyptian doctor might approach a typical situation:

REMEDY FOR A WOUND, THE FIRST DAY

Fat from an ox so that (the wound) may rot, or meat of an ox. But if the wound rots too much then bind on it spoiled barley-bread, so that it may dry. But if (the wound) closes over its secretions, thou shouldst bandage it with grease . . . and crushed peas. If (the wound) beneath breaks open, then powder it with powder of green frit; then bandage it . . . If thereafter (the wound) has covered itself, then make an ointment to strengthen the blood vessels; therewith bandage it, so that it is cured. If thereafter it closes up over its secretions, then prepare: grease, [a plant]; therewith it is bandaged, so that it opens its mouth, so that it rots. It is good for a wound to rot a little. Some wounds may close too early, while there is still rot inside. Therefore, put something on the wound that will get out that rot.

Like their Mesopotamian counterparts, the Egyptian practitioners also believed that ill health was primarily caused by external factors — hence the idea that it was "good for a wound to rot a little," a notion that became the basis for one of the most pervasive, long-lived, and utterly misguided medical doctrines: *pus bonum et laudabile*, "good and laudable pus." Instead of understanding pus to be a by-product of infection, it was seen as the infection itself. Seeing discharge emanate from an injury meant, to Western doctors from Egypt to England, that the body was ridding itself of the cause of the problem.

The Egyptians were primarily concerned with pharmacological solutions to their maladies, and they used a diverse and impressive range of about 700 substances. Among many with dubious medical efficacy — among them dung, ibex grease and turpentine — it appears that they were also early and enthusiastic users of "red shepenn," a plant that archaeologists have now identified as the opium poppy. It was likely imported from Cyprus and, unlike many of the other ingredients they used, its effects were clear: opium is the basis for morphine, a powerful narcotic.

So among the many significant cultural contributions of the ancient Egyptians to the world, perhaps their most profound medical legacy is a single-minded focus on the external causes of poor health and an emphasis on using drugs to alleviate the symptoms. Sound familiar?

The physician's oath

To appreciate the impact of the final ancient Western medical system, you need go no further than the nearest clinic. Odds are good that in at least one of the doctors' offices you'll find hanging on the wall a plaque with these words:

I swear by Apollo Physician and Asclepius and Health and Panacea and all the gods and goddesses, making them witnesses, that I will make complete this oath and this written covenant according to my ability and discernment:

I will use diets for the assistance of the sick according to my ability and discernment; but also to keep away injury of health and injustice.

I will neither give any deadly drug, having been asked for it, nor will I guide the same advice. In purity and in holiness I will maintain my life and my art.

I will not use the knife, not even on those suffering from the stone, but I will give way to those who are practitioners of this work.

And as many houses as I may go into, I will go in for the assistance of the sick, being free from all voluntary injustice and mischief and the rest . . .

That which I may see or hear during treatment, or even outside of treatment concerning the life of men, which must not in any way be divulged outside, I will not speak, regarding such things to be unutterable.

And so may it be to me making complete my oath and not making it of no effect that I enjoy the benefits of my life and art and be honored by all men for time eternal; but may it be the opposite of this to me transgressing and swearing falsely.

The American Medical Association has condensed the original and made it a little more reader-friendly, and it is this version that is most often displayed in modern physicians' offices:

You do solemnly swear, each by whatever he or she holds most sacred:

1. That you will be loyal to the Profession of Medicine and just and generous to its members.

2. That you will lead your lives and practice your art in uprightness and honor.

3. That into whatsoever house you shall enter, it shall be for the good of the sick to the utmost of your power, your holding yourselves far aloof from wrong, from corruption, from the tempting of others to vice.

4. That you will exercise your art solely for the cure of your patients, and will give no drug, perform no operation, for a criminal purpose, even if solicited, far less suggest it.

5. That whatsoever you shall see or hear of the lives of men

*or women which is not fitting to be spoken, you will keep
inviolably secret.*

*These things do you swear. Let each bow the head in sign of
acquiescence. And now, if you will be true to this, your oath,
may prosperity and good repute be ever yours; the opposite, if
you shall prove yourselves forsworn.*

Ironically, several historians now doubt that these words — the famous Hippocratic Oath — were quite as important in pre-Christian Greece as they became in later years. Still, there is no question that Hippocratic physicians profoundly shaped medical practice and philosophy up until comparatively recent times.

So who was Hippocrates? From what we know, he was born around 460 B.C. on Cos, an island located off the coast of what is now Turkey. He was from a medical family; his father was a physician-priest in the cult of Asclepius. Upon entering practice himself, though, Hippocrates began to rethink how Greek medicos approached illness.

Most Greek physicians were members of the Cnidian school, which saw the body as a collection of isolated parts. Accordingly, when things went wrong with a particular organ, they tended to treat it in isolation. To diagnose disease, they relied almost entirely on the patient's own subjective account of his or her symptoms.

Hippocrates brought Greek logic to bear on the problem, preferring to collect objective data about the signs and symptoms of disease. That also allowed a more consistent and rigorous classification of disorders, many of which are ring familiar to modern ears: asthma, arthritis, sepsis, hypochondria, to name just a few.

Hippocrates also rejected the disease-in-isolation approach of the Cnidians. He formulated the theory that the human body was an integrated whole — a *physis* — and should be treated as such. He advanced the theory of the "four humors" to create a new conceptual framework: health is a harmonious balance of these four humors, while disease results from any imbalance to them. The physician's job is to use his art to restore that balance. In Hippocrates' own words:

> The body of man has in itself blood, phlegm, yellow bile, and black bile; these make up the nature of the body, and through these he feels pain or enjoys health. Now, he enjoys the most perfect health when these elements are duly proportioned to one another in respect to compounding, power and bulk, and when they are perfectly mingled. Pain is felt when one of these elements is in defect or excess, or is isolated in the body without being compounded with all the others.

Each humor was associated with a season, an element, and certain signal qualities, as the table below shows:

Blood	Phlegm	Yellow Bile	Black Bile
Spring	Winter	Summer	Autumn
Air	Water	Fire	Earth
Hot and moist	Cold and moist	Hot and dry	Cold and dry

Once he had identified which of the four humors was out of whack, the Hippocratic physician would generally prescribe a regimen of diet, activity and exercise to try and restore the body's natural balance. For example, if the patient was suffering from a fever — a hot, dry disease — the obvious cause was an excess of yellow bile. To counteract its effects, the doctor would try to increase its opposite humor, phlegm, by prescribing a series of cold baths. On the other hand, if the patient was suffering from a cold (an obvious excess of phlegm!) the physician would usually order the patient to bundle up in bed and drink wine.

The Hippocratic school revolutionized Western medicine, removing it further from the magical remedies of the Egyptians and Mesopotamians. By viewing the body as a closed system and applying the principles of Aristotelian logic to the diagnosis of disease, Hippocratic physicians laid the foundation for modern medical science. The principles established by Hippocrates and refined by Galen remained dominant in Europe and later America until the late eighteenth century, when Enlightenment-era anatomists and physicians began to formulate a whole new approach to health: germ theory.

Yin and yang

At almost the same historical moment that the Hippocratic school flourished in the West, an unknown scribe (or scribes) far to the east produced the most important medical text in Chinese history: the *Huangdi Neijing* (roughly translated as "Manual of Physic"). Its contrast to any of the Western texts we have examined is immediate and striking; rather than a list of prescriptions, it takes the form of a dialogue between the emperor, Huang Ti, and his prime minister, Ch'i Po. Ch'i Po never presents himself as a physician, and his advice is highly philosophical rather than strictly practical. In one example, for instance, he is more concerned with guiding the patient back to Tao — "The Way" — then giving him specific directions about how to treat his diarrhea.

Chinese medicine concerned itself less with treating the physical symptoms of an ailment than discovering how the complementary universal duality between elements of darkness (*yin*) and light (*yang*) had become skewed within the body itself and then restoring it to its proper harmonic balance. Unlike Western physicians, who looked for physical causes to ailments, Chinese healers operated first and foremost from a philosophical, spiritual perspective:

> When the spirit is hurt, severe pains ensue; where the body
> is hurt, there will be swellings. Thus, in those cases where
> severe pains are felt first and the swellings appear later, one
> can say that the spirit has injured the body. And in those

cases where swellings appear first and severe pains are felt later, one can say that the body has injured the spirit.

Ch'i Po answered: "The utmost in the art of healing can be achieved when there is unity."

The Emperor inquired: "What is meant by unity?"

Ch'i Po answered: "When the minds of the people are closed and wisdom is locked out they remain tied to disease. Yet their feelings and desires should be investigated and made known, their wishes and ideas should be followed; and then it becomes apparent that those who have attained spirit and energy are flourishing and prosperous, while those perish who lose their spirit and energy."

Life itself is the beginning of illness.

Surgery is never mentioned in the *Huangdi Neijing*, and drugs are just hinted at. The one course of treatment discussed in detail is acupuncture, which was designed to channel the body's vital energy, or *ch'i*, through vessels called "meridians." On one level, this was a subtler version of the Greco-Roman emphasis on bloodletting; by needling the right meridian, *ch'i* could be drawn off where an imbalance existed. Unlike the Western practice, however, *ch'i* could also be directed inward, or replenished, by accessing another meridian. Modern acupuncturists still sometimes use the terms "disperse" and "tonify" to describe the dual purpose of their craft. According to one of those modern acupuncturists, "the vital energy of the body is the same energy that fills the cosmos."

Besides acupuncture, ancient Chinese physicians — like their Hippocratic counterparts — also prescribed changes in diet and activity for their patients. Fortunately for Chinese patients, these remedies tended to be rather milder than the ice baths and purgative regimens that Greek patients frequently endured. More fundamentally, they were intended to restore the sufferer's harmonic relationship to the universe, not simply correct a purely physical ailment.

The science of life

As we finish our whirlwind tour of the ancient world's great medical traditions, our final stop is the vast subcontinent of India. Some three and a half thousand years ago, a group of people called the Aryans overran the indigenous cultures and subsequently produced a civilization rich in art, religion and literature. The initial basis for that cultural flowering was four sacred texts, or Vedas, that the newcomers either brought with them or produced soon thereafter from an extensive and meticulous oral tradition.

The fourth of those texts, the Atharva Veda, gave rise to a system of medical thought called Ayurveda, literally the "science of life." By the eighth century B.C., a trio of foundational Ayurvedic medical texts had been written: the *Charak Samhita*, the *Sushurta Samhita,* and the *Ashtanga Hridaya*. These books described the basic principles which have endured into the present day.

Superficially, the Ayurvedic view of the body resembles that of the ancient Greeks, in that both traditions viewed the body's substances as reflecting the elements of the natural world. But unlike Hippocratic physicians, practitioners of Ayurveda believed that those elements combined within the body into three *doshas*, or principles: Vata (wind), Pitta (fire) and Kapha (earth). Each individual possesses a unique combination of these *doshas* that defines his or her innate mental and physical temperament: their *prakriti*. Although all three are present in everyone, usually one or two *doshas* is predominant.

Those people in which Vata is the dominant *dosha* tend to be thin, enthusiastic, energetic, and changeable. If Pitta is predominates, a person is usually intense, intelligent, and goal-oriented. If Kapha is the strongest *dosha*, the individual is usually easy-going, methodical, and nurturing.

Poor health results when a person's *prakriti* becomes imbalanced. For example, if Vata becomes too dominant, a person can experience anxiety, insomnia, dry skin, constipation, and difficulty focusing. When Pitta is out of balance, a person can become compulsive, irritable and suffer from indigestion. If Kapha becomes imbalanced, a person may experience sluggishness, weight gain and sinus congestion.

The goal of Ayurveda is to identify a person's ideal state of balance, and then determine if and where an imbalance exists. If the *prakriti* is imbalanced, a combination of diet, herbs, aromatherapy, massage treatments, music and meditation can be used to reestablish balance and restore the individual to full health. Ayurveda places great importance on one's *pathya*, or lifestyle. Diet is particularly significant; in the words of an Ayurvedic proverb: "When diet is wrong, medicine is of no use. When diet is correct, medicine is of no need."

In the event of a physical injuries, ancient Ayurvedic physicians were proficient in treating everything from war wounds to hunting accidents. They also, believe or not, were the best plastic surgeons of the ancient world — ancient texts detail how to repair torn earlobes and even reconstruct mutilated noses. Some of the techniques are remarkably similar to ones used by modern doctors.

It should also be noted that Ayurvedic practices are still used by hundreds of millions of patients as well, from India to Europe to the United States. As even Hippocrates himself once noted, "Foolish the doctor who despises the knowledge acquired by the ancients."

Eastern approaches

If your head is spinning a little trying to assimilate all this information about these very different medical traditions, that's understandable. Let's try to simplify things a bit by identifying the major contrasts between the traditional Western approach to medicine with the Eastern models.

All of the three early Western schools of thought — Mesopotamian, Egyptian and Greco-Roman — viewed disease as a result of purely physical causes stemming from outside the body. Curing ill health meant ridding the body of those noxious substances, through primitive pharmaceuticals, surgery or purging. If the disease could not be cured, at least drugs might help manage the sufferer's symptoms.

In stark contrast, both the Chinese and the Ayurvedic schools emphasize a holistic approach that encompasses the spiritual as well as the physical. Poor health is a result of some sort of physical/spiritual/mental imbalance in the patient, and the goal of Eastern practitioners is to restore that balance through a combination of generally non-invasive techniques.

As Dr. Julia Tsuei succinctly puts it, "The development of medicine in Western nations follows the way of hypothetical deduction and the Eastern approach uses the inductive method. The Western approach clearly divides the health from the disease, yet the Eastern approach considers health as a balanced state versus disease as an unbalanced state. The Western approach tends to change the environment and the Eastern way is to prefer to adapt to the environment."

While the Western model does many things well, it is also inherently limited — especially when it comes to treating many of the chronic conditions brought on or accentuated by our modern, hectic, unbalanced lives. We gravitate to Western approaches because they promise a quick fix, one that doesn't require us to really address the underlying issues of our poor health. Dr. Rachel Naomi Remen, who has developed the Commonweal Retreat Center for cancer patients, described it well: "*Helping, fixing* and *serving* represent three different ways of seeing life. When you help, you see life as weak. When you fix, you see life as broken. When you serve, you see life as whole. Fixing and helping may be the work of the ego, and service the work of the soul."

For all its technological acumen and pharmaceutical prowess, modern Western medicine has constricted its focus to purely a cure-oriented, "fixing" model. And if it can't fix the problem, at least it can temporarily fix the symptoms. That's why the pharmaceutical business is booming — at the first sign of discomfort, we run to the medicine cabinet to pop a pill. Can't remember whether you're supposed to starve a cold or feed a fever? Heck, just swallow some antibiotics and Tylenol and head off to work or school.

Not only is this a short-sighted approach, it can be a dangerous one. In his book *The Gift of Pain*, Dr. Paul Brand recounts his experiences treating victims of Hansen's Disease — commonly known as leprosy — in both the United States and India. For thousands of years, lepers have been relegated to the fringes of society, made outcasts because their hideous deformities inspired fear and revulsion even in family and friends. Jewish audiences hearing the Gospel of Matthew's account of Jesus healing a leper by *touching* him would likely have been scandalized; doing so was a major taboo.

What Brand discovered, however, is that it's not the disease itself that directly causes these deformities. Hansen's Disease actually affects the nerves, causing the body's pain receptors to stop functioning. Without pain, victims of leprosy are unaware of injury and infection — a grain of dust in the eye, instead of triggering the eye to water and the eyelid to blink rapidly, simply goes unnoticed and eventually causes real damage. Over time, repeated incidents like this can lead to blindness. By the same process, a small cut can lead to a limb-threatening infection.

Pain, then, is not so much something to be *avoided* as something to be *heeded*. Traditional Eastern cultures generally adopt a view closer to this perspective, emphasizing that pain is a signal that the individual's spiritual and physical being are out of balance. The pain itself is not what's significant; what's important is the ability to look past it to understand the root causes.

In the next couple of chapters, we'll examine the very real links between our emotional, mental, physical and spiritual states. We'll see how one impacts the others, and you'll begin to understand why we need an alternative approach — a new mindset — in order to achieve and sustain true health.

Chapter Three

The Mind-Body Connection

*"Change happens for you the moment you want something
more than you fear it."*

-Eric Micha'el Leventhal

S everal years ago I saw a patient — for the sake of anonymity, let's call him Jake — who came to me complaining of frequent low back pain. Although he was approaching his mid-60s, Jake to most outward appearances seemed to be in good health for his age. He wasn't overweight, he was physically and mentally active, and by most measures he had lived a remarkable and successful life. He had built a multi-million dollar company from the ground up and enjoyed the perks of wealth.

Soon I discovered that lower back issues were just the tip of the iceberg for Jake. He also complained of frequent insomnia, low energy, digestive problems, and a whole host of other troubles. Interestingly, none of these maladies had appeared until relatively recently. He had gone to a number of doctors, general practitioners and specialists alike, and none of them had discovered anything amiss.

At first, Jake liked to impress me with accounts of his jet-setting lifestyle: "So, I was in Hong Kong over the weekend . . ." and "You'll never guess who I had dinner with last week . . ." Over the course of his treatment, however, he (like many of my patients) began to open up about his seemingly perfect life — which, as it turns out, wasn't as perfect as he liked to pretend.

The truth is that Jake was contemplating his imminent retirement, and that he was deeply conflicted about it. He had poured his entire adult life into his business. He was a self-professed workaholic with few outside interests. Both his parents had died at a relatively early age. He had never married, never had children. Although frequently accompanied by beautiful companions on his many travels and surrounded by a small army of employees, associates and business contacts, he had few (if any) deep friendships. Everything in his life revolved around the company he had built.

"I'm afraid," he finally confessed. "I don't think I can stop working. What will I do with my life?"

It became clear that this mentally brilliant man was also an emotionally and spiritually immature human being, something most people who encountered him never realized. Apart from business, he had no purpose, no belief in anything beyond himself. Intellectually, he knew that there was a void in his life, but he didn't understand how to fill it except to pour everything into the one area in which he excelled.

Several months after I initially saw him, Jake did retire . . . sort of. He gave up operational control of the company, but stayed on the executive board in order to continue to provide "big picture" guidance. He pitched it as a way to help ease the transition in leadership, but we both knew the truth: he just couldn't walk away from the only thing in his life that gave it meaning.

About a year later, Jake dropped dead from a massive heart attack. There had been no overt warning signs, no discernible physical reason why this seemingly healthy man had suddenly keeled over. They were puzzled, but wrote it off as "just one of those things."

The power of positivity

To me the cause of Jake's death was no mystery. Understanding it, though, required a non-Western approach to health and disease, something neither his doctors nor Jake himself was able to embrace. Jake suffered from a profound imbalance in the spiritual and emotional aspects of his being, an imbalance which manifested itself in an escalating series of physical symptoms: back pain, insomnia, gastric distress. His physicians had searched only for a *physical* cause to those physical symptoms and, finding none, had simply tried to treat the symptoms themselves while reassuring him that "there was nothing to worry about."

In retrospect, clearly there had been something to worry about. Those physical symptoms were Jake's body trying to send him a wake-up call, to prompt him to make the changes needed for real health. In his case, his fear of losing his purpose in life was likely the root cause of what eventually killed him. "Over the years I've learned that there are really just two mental patterns that contribute to disease: fear and anger," says self-help guru Louise Hay. "Anger can show up as impatience, irritation, frustration, criticism, resentment, jealousy or bitterness. Fear could be tension, anxiety, nervousness, worry, doubt, feeling not good enough or unworthiness. These are all thoughts that poison the body. When we release this burden, all the organs in our body begin to function properly."

Louise is one of the modern pioneers in this approach to medicine, connecting illness to corresponding non-physical trigger factors. Her first book, *Heal Your Body*, has been translated into 25 languages and sold more than 40 million copies since its publication in 1976. She has also been a catalyst for helping a new generation of "whole health" practitioners like Deepak Chopra and Wayne Dyer reach an audience.

Louise's philosophy of health was a long time coming. Her early life was the stuff of a Lifetime Network movie: poverty, physical abuse and rape. She eventually ran away to New York City and became a successful model, eventually marrying a prosperous executive. That outward success only served to mask the dysfunction beneath, and it wasn't until her marriage ended a decade and a half later that she really began to heal.

In the 1970s she began training in the ministerial program of the Church of Religious Science. She soon became both a popular speaker at the church and a sought-after counselor. Her experiences helped her see recurring patterns in how physical ailments were often the result of mental, emotional and spiritual causes. She developed the "Heal Your Life" program, an approach to reversing illness and creating health by developing overriding positive thought patterns to deal with the unresolved underlying causes of disease. Participants learn how to use a variety of techniques —

including positive affirmations and mirror work — to release the negative emotions that block joy and creativity.

In the late 1970s, Louise contracted a rare, deadly form of cervical cancer. After diagnosing the source of the cancer as her own resentment about her childhood traumas, she rejected traditional surgery and drugs to treat what doctors had told her was an effectively "incurable" disease. She instead began a regimen of affirmations, visualization, nutritional cleansing, reflexology and psychotherapy to allow her to forgive those who had abused her and release the negativity caused by her emotional baggage.

Six months later, Louise was cancer free.

My first exposure to Louise Hay was shortly after my high school graduation when a family friend gave me a copy of her book, *You Can Heal Your Life*. It was unlike anything I'd ever read, and it prompted me to begin to look at health and happiness in a completely new way. As I progressed through my undergraduate studies, unsure exactly what I wanted to do with my life but certain that I wanted to help people, I branched out into many of the other authors Louise has inspired and supported throughout her career. Through them I began to gain insights into why people became ill, as well as why some others suddenly experienced spontaneous, seemingly miraculous remissions or healings of serious diseases. More than simply an intellectual exercise, I began gradually incorporating her exercises into my own life.

When I finally began seeing patients of my own in chiropractic practice, I saw Louise's philosophy of health validated time and again with surprising consistency. Patients who came in complaining of migraines were, as it turned out, frequently wrestling with some big, difficult life decision. Others who came in because of lower back pain were often going through breakups or divorces or dealing with bankruptcy issues. As a result, I began seeing people as much, much more than simply a physical body. To achieve real healing — as Louise did with her cancer — it was critical that we expand our medical horizons to deal with the whole spectrum of body, mind, emotion and spirit.

Death of an icon

Contrast Louise Hay's example with that of Steve Jobs, who died at the age of 56 of pancreatic cancer. Jobs left behind an entrepreneurial legacy to be reckoned with: co-founder of Apple and Pixar, developer of the Macintosh personal computer, the iPod, the iPad and the iPhone. Without question, Jobs changed the way the world interacts with technology.

But beyond the products themselves, Jobs had an at times tumultuous personal and professional life; colleagues often accused him of being more marketer than inventor. "Steve didn't ever code," recalled Apple co-founder Steve Wozniak. "He wasn't an engineer and he didn't do any original design." Daniel Kottke, one of Apple's earliest employees, also dismissed Jobs's technical prowess: "Between Woz and Jobs, Woz was the innovator, the inventor. Steve Jobs was the marketing person."

By most accounts, Jobs was a difficult, perfectionist boss, often demanding that employees "drink the Kool-Aid" by working 100-hour weeks and refraining from any sort of perceived criticism. Apple's third co-founder, Ronald Wayne, described him as a cold, ruthless businessman who once asked Wayne to convince a friend to sell his company for Apple's benefit. He seemed to need to be the smartest guy in the room; according to biographer Walter Isaacson, he once berated President Obama for the shortage of software engineers and told the president that he was "headed for a one-term presidency." When he felt his proposed solutions to the problem were not being taking seriously, Jobs complained, "The president is very smart, but he kept explaining to us reasons why things can't get done. It infuriates me."

In 1993 Jobs made *Fortune*'s list of "America's Toughest Bosses." Dan'l Lewin co-founded NeXT Inc. with Jobs after he was ousted from Apple in 1985 following a power struggle with CEO John Sculley, whom he had personally recruited from Pepsi-Cola just two years previously. Recalled Lewin, "The highs were unbelievable, but the lows were unimaginable." Even after returning to Apple in 1997, Jobs showed that he hadn't mellowed — according to an article on Salon.com, many employees were reluctant to ride in the same elevator, afraid that they might not have a job when the doors opened. The reality was that Jobs's summary executions were rare, but a handful of victims was enough to terrorize a whole company."

For all of Steve Jobs's brilliance, that streak of ruthlessness and lack of empathy signifies a major emotional imbalance, one that seems to have been present from an early age. While working for Atari in the mid-70s, Jobs was assigned to create a circuit board for the Breakout arcade game. Atari had offered $100 for each chip that could be eliminated, so Jobs approached Wozniak and offered to split the fee with him. Much to everyone's amazement, Woz was able to cut 50 chips. Jobs collected the $5000, then told Wozniak that Atari had decided to only give them $700. He gave his partner $350 and pocketed the rest, something Wozniak didn't discover until a decade later.

Could that emotional imbalance have contributed to the cancer that caused Steve Jobs's death? It's impossible to make a second-hand diagnosis, but I wouldn't rule it out. Based on Louise Hay's experience, she says that the pancreas represents sweetness in life; cancer is often a physical manifestation of deep hurt and long-standing resentment. Pancreatic dysfunction, then, is a result of an inability to "digest" the richness of life because of some emotional or spiritual blockage.

"Anger turns into things that boil and burn and infect the body," Hay cautions. "Resentment long held festers and eats away at the self and ultimately can lead to tumors and cancer. Guilt always seeks punishment and leads to pain."

The mind-body connection

What Louise Hay observed — and what I've seen confirmed again and again in my own years of practice — is that negative emotions without a doubt render the body susceptible to disease and dysfunction. Memory patterns of unresolved prior emotional traumas can and do lead to very real, very measurable — and sometimes potentially very dangerous — health crises.

Interestingly, there's often a specific correlation about what physical ailments are caused by specific mental/emotional root causes. Low back issues, for instance, are frequently the result of financial anxiety. What we usually diagnose as a cold generally stems from the patient feeling overwhelmed by events or unable to keep up with an overabundance of commitments. Even asthma can be brought on by a sense of being stifled or smothered; the inability to "breathe" emotionally manifests itself as an actual physical inability to breathe.

I remember one patient who was afflicted by severe migraines. The attacks increased in frequency, intensity and duration to the point that she was virtually unable to lead a normal life. She lived in constant fear of what might trigger another migraine, and it affected every aspect of her life, professional and personal. She had consulted with many doctors in the couple of years before I saw her, but all had come away stumped. She had submitted to repeated MRIs and all sorts of tests, but no one could find a physiological reason for her headaches. In desperation, she had resorted to simply trying to manage the migraines through a variety of pain-relieving pharmaceuticals — which, in turn, caused other negative side effects.

Finally, we were able to ascertain that the real cause of the headaches was an unresolved conflict she was feeling over a career choice she had made years before. The resulting stress, instead of dissipating over time, had actually snowballed until it began to affect her physically. And here's what's truly astounding: for years she had absolutely no idea what was really causing the migraines!

Your brain and you

To fully appreciate why our non-physical nature has so much power over our physical selves, let's step back and consider the human brain. Frankly, it's not much to look at: a ridged, gelatinous-looking loaf that weighs about three pounds in an adult. The ancient Egyptians and early Greeks we discussed in the last chapter regarded the heart, not the brain, as the seat of memory and consciousness.

What they had no way of knowing is just what an amazing organ it really is: 100 billion nerve cells, or *neurons*, each of which is capable of making contact with thousands — or even tens of thousands — of other neurons through tiny structures called synapses. In the time it took you to read that last sentence, your brain formed probably close to *seven million* new connections, each of which had a unique pattern.

There are several different types of neurons, some of which are very specialized. Besides neurons, your brain contains *glial cells* that amplify neural signals; scientists estimate that we have about ten times as many glial cells as neurons. Up until fairly recently, scientists believed that brain cells were created only during childhood, but now we know that *neurogenesis* —new cells being born — occurs throughout our lives. The brain seems to have growth bursts, after which it takes a little while to consolidate the new cells and "prune" excess connections. The most notable bursts happen during the first couple of years of life and again during puberty/young adulthood. If you've ever marveled at how easily children seem to be able to learn another language while you've struggled to do it as an adult, that's the reason.

Structurally, the brain is divided into two *cerebral hemispheres*, right and left. The cerebrum is, in evolutionary terms, the most recent brain structure. Besides being the largest, it also deals with the most complex cognitive activities. At the risk of grossly oversimplifying things, the right hemisphere handles the more creative, emotional and intuitive aspects of cognition; the left focuses on language and logic.

Near the back of the cerebrum are the *occipital lobe*, which controls vision, and (above it) the *parietal lobe*, which deals with movement, orientation and calculation. Behind the ears and temples we find the two *temporal lobes*, which process sound and speech comprehension. At the front of the cerebrum are the *frontal* and *prefrontal lobes*, which handle our most complex cognitive functions: planning, abstract thought, conceptualization, attention control, decision making, and higher order social emotions like regret and empathy. This area is sometimes also classified as the *sensory cortex* and the *motor cortex*, which together are responsible for controlling incoming information and regulating outgoing behavior.

Beneath the forebrain we find more evolutionarily primitive regions, especially the *limbic system*. Common to all mammals, the structures of the limbic system deal with urges and appetites. Strong primal emotions are most closely linked to the *amygdala, caudate nucleus* and *putamen*. Within the limbic region we also find the *thalamus*, which serves as a kind of sensory relay station; the *hypothalamus*, which releases key hormones; and the *hippocampus*, which is essential in the forming of new memories.

Behind the cerebrum is a smaller region called the *cerebellum*, which is responsible for storing patterns of repeated movement — basically all those tasks we can literally do without consciously thinking about. Beneath the cerebellum lie the most primitive parts of the brain, the midbrain and the brain stem, which control the body's autonomic functions (those we have no conscious control over) like breathing, heart rate, blood pressure, digestion, sleep patterns, etc.

Conscious vs. subconscious

Another way to think about, well, *how* we think is to divide cognition into the *conscious* and *unconscious* mind. The former describes all the processes we have deliberate, intentional control over; the latter describes everything else that our brain does. Let's discuss the conscious mind first.

The cortex is the part of the brain associated with the activities of our conscious mind. Although it is the largest segment of the brain and, in evolutionary terms, the "new brain," it actually controls less than 10 percent of our cognitive function — pretty much the rational, decision-making tasks. It relies heavily on objective sensory input and language, and is firmly rooted in present time stimuli and voluntary actions. Most of our short-term memory seems to be connected to the conscious mind.

The subconscious mind, in contrast, controls more than 90% of our brain's daily activity. It comprises the more primitive parts of the brain (the limbic system and hindbrain), relying on emotions and feelings and controlling a whole range of involuntary reactions. If you've ever experienced the "fight or flight" phenomenon, that's your subconscious at work. If you've ever awakened from a nightmare with your heart racing and your hair slicked with sweat, that's your subconscious at work, too. Unlike the conscious mind, it isn't bound by the "here and now," which is why those naked-in-front-of-the-whole-class dreams can be so powerful . . . even years after you've graduated. In fact, several studies increasingly suggest that most of our long-term memory is diffused throughout various parts of the subconscious.

Here's the problem: our conscious mind doesn't even *begin* developing until sometime between the ages of three and six, and doesn't finish its development until around 20 years of age. That means that during our most formative years, when we're soaking up experiences and information, we lack the analytical filter to rationally process them, prioritize them and gauge their impact.

That's why seemingly innocuous stimuli — smells, textures, sounds — can suddenly evoke powerful and unlooked-for memories. It's why certain phrases can bring back feelings of childhood inferiority or helplessness, why it's so difficult to let go of past hurts and resentments. So much of who we are is built on the foundation of our subconscious and, particularly in times of stress, it easily overrides our conscious intentions and prompts us to react emotionally. All of us have a myriad of counterproductive subconscious "programs," many of them established before our conscious mind finished developing, that in turn hinder our ability to live our lives to their fullest, happiest and healthiest.

In my practice, I've seen many patients suffering from sometimes extreme and debilitating conditions that we were eventually able to trace back to this type of subconscious imbalance. One memorable example was a young man who without warning began suffering from severe seizures. Like many of my patients, to the casual eye it seemed that he had a perfect life: high-paying job, lovely wife, palatial house. Only after several months of treatment were we able to finally ascertain that he was struggling to live up to a definition of success that had been "programmed" into him throughout his childhood and adolescence. Trying to measure up to that externally-generated standard created an internal conflict between what he "had" to do and what he really, in his heart of hearts, "wanted" to do. His mind's inability to reconcile this contradiction ultimately resulted in a very real, very dangerous physical condition.

The good news is that it is possible to reprogram aspects of our subconscious mind through techniques such as visualization. At the most recent winter Olympics, for instance, the U.S. team brought along nine sports psychologists to help the athletes imagine not only the steps required for a successful event, but even experiential details, goes beyond "visualization" in her training. "You have to smell it," said Emily Cook, a veteran U.S. freestyle aerialist. "You have to hear it. You have to feel it, everything."

Cook even used visualization to help speed her recovery from a gruesome injury in 2002, when she broke bones in both her feet. Working with Nicole Detling, a noted sports psychologist, she used imagery to see and feel her bones heal. The technique worked so well that Cook began incorporating it into her regular training.

According to an article in *The New York Times*:

> (Cook and Detling) created imagery scripts, highly detailed written accounts of the competition process from "Point A to Point Z." Each jump sequence lasts about 10 seconds but packs a great deal of action into that small window, particularly in the air with the flipping and spinning. But Cook broke it all down and then recorded the script.
>
> "I would say into the recorder: 'I'm standing on the top of the hill. I can feel the wind on the back of my neck. I can hear the crowd,' " Cook said. "Kind of going through all those different senses and then actually going through what I wanted to do for the perfect jump. I turn down the in-run. I stand up. I engage my core. I look at the top of the jump.
> "I was going through every little step of how I wanted that jump to turn out."
>
> Cook then played the recording back as she relaxed, eyes closed, feeling her muscles firing in response. She said

that such mental work helped her return to the sport a better jumper and that she also had used imagery to break the cycle of negativity. Whenever fear surfaced, she would picture herself pricking a big red balloon with a pin.

Even if the situation doesn't lend itself to visualization strategies, it's still possible to align your conscious and subconscious perspectives. Sometimes, it's simply a matter of recognizing the source of the dysfunction and facing it head-on. The young executive I mentioned finally brought his seizures under control (and eventually eliminated them entirely) by coming to terms with the fact that, ultimately, his parents' vision of a successful life didn't match his own. Through a combination of lifestyle changes (leaving his job for a lower-paying but more fulfilling one) and re-focusing techniques (regular daily meditation), he became healthier — and happier — than he'd ever been.

In Chapter Seven, we'll discuss more tools and techniques you can use to improve your health by taking out the negative trash that litters your subconscious mind and sabotages your health. But first we have one final but vitally important area of health to consider: your spiritual health.

Chapter Four

The Search for Balance

"Your sacred space is where you can find yourself over and over again."

-Joseph Campbell

O nce upon a time there was a very angry woman. Her temper tantrums terrorized her family and neighbors, who quickly learned the necessity of walking on eggshells in their dealings with her. Even then, though, none of them knew when an ill-considered word or an untimely — even accidental — action would result in a volcanic explosion.

As the years passed, the woman's temper only grew worse. She seemed perpetually angry. And while those closest to her suffered the most, the boundaries of her rage gradually expanded to include everyone in her village, passing travelers, even animals. Then she began to rail against inanimate objects: a squeaky door, a drafty window, a slightly crooked flagstone on the path.

Her anger even turned against nature itself. When it rained, she cursed the clouds for ruining her laundry day. When the sun shined, she cursed it for causing her to squint. There was no pleasing her: spring was too wet, summer too hot, autumn too windy, winter too cold. To enter her field of vision was to become a target for her venomous rage.

Eventually, the other villagers had had enough. Individually, they were all terrified of her, so they planned to confront her as a group. Summoning their collective courage, they demanded that for the sake of peace she leave the village and not return until she had found a cure for the anger that consumed her.

For years the woman wandered the land. Her sorrow only fueled the fires of her rage. Birds hushed their singing at her approach, and flowers turned their bright faces from her. Even her shadow strayed as far from her as it dared.

One day, she heard about a wise man who was reputed to be able to cure any malady. "My rage has gained me nothing and cost me everything," she said to herself. "Perhaps he can take it from me and I can return to my home and my family."

So she made the arduous journey to the wise man's dwelling, far away in the mountains. She arrived in a foul mood, thirsty, tired, and much bruised from the climb. She saw the old man sitting on the stoop of his hut, silently watching her approach. The sight of him caused her temper to flare, and she blasted him for building his home in such an inaccessible spot, for not taking the time to clear a better path, for sitting idly by while poor travelers risked life and limb.

The wise man sat and said nothing.

That only increased the woman's rage. She insulted his appearance, his reputation, and his parentage. She demanded that he pay attention to her.

The wise man stood up and walked into his hut.

Infuriated now to a level rare even for her, she stormed into the hut after him . . . only to hear the door shut and lock behind her. The wise man stood outside the hut, gazing silently at the woman through a small window. The woman screamed and banged on the door, but it didn't budge. Finally, exhausted, she sank to the ground.

"You are like a kettle of boiling water," the wise man said softly into the silence. "You are in constant motion, constant opposition to yourself. You are not in balance." And he left.

Days passed, and finally the wise man appeared again at the window. This time, instead of screaming, the woman's response was haughty: "I have changed my mind. I no longer need your assistance. Release me so I may be on my way."

"You are like a block of ice," the wise man said softly. "You have no flexibility, no capacity to adapt to change. You are not in balance." And he left.

When he returned days later, the woman reacted tearfully. "Please,

please let me leave," she begged. "I've learned my lesson. I'll never lose my temper again. I'll live in peace with my family and neighbors. I'll be grateful every day for what I have."

"You are like a cloud in the summer sky," the wise man said softly. "You are not grounded. You have no substance, no reality. You are not in balance." And he left.

Many more days passed. Eventually the wise man returned, but the woman didn't notice him — she was staring at a single leaf floating in a nearby puddle. Eventually her gaze turned to the wise man. "I was remembering floating in our village lake as a young girl," she said. "I remember watching the clouds float past, feeling the warmth of the sun and the coolness of the water all at once. It was the last time I truly felt happy."

"That is the essence of contentment," the wise man said, "experiencing each sensation without judging, acknowledging all and judging none, becoming neither too hot or too cold, neither too firm nor too ephemeral."

He unlocked the door. The woman thanked him and returned to her home, no longer mastered by her rage.

Searching for balance

We talk a lot about balance these days: balancing the demands of work with finding time for family and relaxation, balancing the longing for personal space with the desire to give back to the community or to those less fortunate than ourselves, balancing the urge for activity with the need for rest. Channel surf through morning news shows or afternoon talk shows or evening informational shows and you'll find no shortage of segments extolling the need for better balance in our lives, telling us how terrible we Westerners are at finding that balance, and offering a whole raft of solutions ranging from simple "life hacks" to major lifestyle makeovers.

Modern advertising, in fact, absolutely relies on this deeply felt urge to achieve balance, selling everything from SUVs to insurance to energy drinks with the promise — implicit or explicit — that the product in question is the missing piece in our quest for contentment and peace of mind. *If*

I buy this mattress I'll sleep better, and then I'll be more productive at work and have more energy to play with the kids in the evening. If we book this cruise, it'll get us away from the daily grind and recharge our relationship. If I order this juicer, it'll make me eat healthier and I'll feel better about myself.

It's rare, of course, for any of those purchases to fully deliver on that transformative promise. We are creatures of habit, and all too often we simply fall back into whatever familiar groove we generally inhabit.

Crisis can shock us into other patterns of behavior, but even then the effect is often surprisingly temporary. In the immediate wake of the 9/11 attacks, for instance, church and synagogue attendance in the U.S. spiked an estimated 25 percent, causing many pundits to predict a cultural paradigm shift. According to a Barna Group report, however, in less than two months attendance levels had fallen back to levels consistent with the prior year. Some paradigm shift.

Less dramatic examples of the same phenomenon happen each January 1, when millions of people (an estimated 40 percent of Americans) sincerely resolve to make their lives "better" by joining a gym or working fewer weekends or getting organized. But when time management firm FranklinCovey polled more than 15,000 customers, it found that a third of those resolutions were broken by February. A University of Scranton study determined that less than 8 percent of those who made New Year's resolutions successfully kept them for the entire year.

The problem is that in those resolutions we are too often selling ourselves the same bill of goods as advertisers do: that a single change will have sudden, sweeping and sustainable positive benefits. Compounding that is our collective Western preoccupation with that change coming as the result of some sort of external, material stimulus: a new house, a new job, a new wardrobe. We are inevitably disappointed . . . and we almost inevitably fall right back into the same trap, time and again.

That pattern resists even major external stimuli. Consider winning the lottery. On its surface, it would seem the answer to a whole raft of prayers and problems: debt, the constraints of an unsatisfying career, providing for family, etc. But a recent study by the Camelot Group of 34 lottery winners found that almost half reported being no happier than they were before their big win. In fact, 44% of those interviewed had spent all their winnings within five years, overspending on houses, cars, clothes, vacations, jewelry and other things in the hope of finally finding some elusive missing piece to ultimate happiness and contentment.

Several high profile lottery winners exemplify the old maxim that you can't buy happiness. William "Bud" Post, for instance, won a $16.2 million jackpot in Pennsylvania's lottery. He was immediately sued by an ex-girlfriend who claimed (and eventually won) a share of his winnings. After he refused to give his brother any more money, the disgruntled sibling (unsuccessfully) hired a hit man to kill Bud with the idea that he would inherit as a result. Within a few years, Bud was $1 million in debt and filing for bankruptcy. "I wish I would have just torn up that ticket," he is reported to have lamented.

The circle of balance

The problem of balance — and the source of happiness — is nothing new. "Do not spoil what you have by desiring what you have not," cautioned the Greek philosopher Epicurus. "Remember that what you now have was once among the things you only hoped for." Half a world away, the Buddha advised his listeners, "Peace comes from within. Do not seek it without." Two and half millennia later, many of are still struggling — and failing — to follow that advice.

In the last chapter we discussed the influence our minds have over our physiological states, and how imbalances between our conscious and subconscious can lead to very real, very profound health problems. But how do we really bring our mental and physical selves into balance?

One powerful tool is by using the body's *chakras*, an ancient Sanskrit word that means "wheel" or "circle." There are seven main chakras aligned from the base of the spine to the top of the head. They are part of what we call the subtle, or non-physical body, and function as nodes in the system of energy channels through which our *prana*, our life force, flows. When prana energy becomes blocked in a chakra, it can trigger physical, mental, or emotional imbalances that in turn manifest in symptoms such as fatigue, high blood pressure, digestive problems and many more. On the other hand, by properly aligning these seven chakras, you can vitalize your physical body by bringing structure and balance to your mental, emotional and spiritual states as well.

Originally mentioned in the Upanishads, sacred Hindu texts that date back more than 2500 years, each chakra is associated with both an element in nature, a symbolic color, a range of positive and negative emotions and (if blocked) a set of potential physical maladies. Taken together, our chakras provide a diagnostic map of our bodies, helping target the specific source of imbalance.

For example, if you are experiencing stomach ulcers or digestive ailments, we might start by focusing on the third chakra (also known as the "solar plexus chakra" because of its location about three inches above the navel at the base of the sternum). When this chakra is in balance, we feel confident and optimistic; when it's out of balance, our self esteem plummets and we become either overly sensitive to criticism or feel the need to be in complete control of every situation.

To better understand the comprehensiveness of this invisible energy system, let's examine the attributes of each chakra in a little more detail . . .

A chakra road map

The first chakra, also known as the "root chakra," is located on the base of the spine. Primarily associated with our spiritual body, it helps connect us to our physical selves. It particularly influences our skeletal structure, our legs and our adrenal glands. When in balance, it imbues feelings of groundedness and physical vitality. When out of balance, we become restless and fearful, often about financial matters. Physical ailments that can result from an imbalance include various types of arthritis, as well as more general feelings of poor health and low energy. The color associated with the first chakra is red.

The second chakra, also known as the "sacral chakra," is located just below the navel. Primarily associated with our emotional body, it governs our emotional, creative, and sexual energies and is connected to our bladder, womb, nervous system, adrenal glands, and sex organs. We feel social, confident, and creative when it's in balance. When it's not, we become either isolated and withdrawn or, alternately, sometimes codependent. Possible physical problems that can result from an imbalanced sacral chakra include low back pain, impotence, prostrate issues, ovarian cysts, and menstrual difficulties. The color associated with the second chakra is orange.

The third, or solar plexus, chakra is our wisdom center, the source of our self-esteem, personal worth and willpower. When we talk about "trusting your gut," we're really referencing the solar plexus chakra and its location in the torso. It is primarily associated with our mental body and, as mentioned in the previous section, when it's in balance we feel positively towards ourselves and others; when it's out of balance we become negative and mistrustful. Because it governs our liver, pancreas, lower back, stomach, and gall bladder, an imbalance in this chakra can lead to ulcers, digestive problems, chronic fatigue, diabetes, and gallstones. The color associated with the third chakra is yellow.

The fourth chakra is known as the "heart chakra." Associated with our spiritual or energetic body, it governs our ability to both give and receive love. People whose heart chakra is balanced are compassionate, nurturing, and generous — these are the folks who just seem to have an aura of peace and harmony. If it becomes imbalanced, however, we become jealous, depressed, or embittered. Often we begin to fear that those close to us will somehow betray our love or trust. It is connected with the heart (naturally), arms, lower lungs, upper back, and the thymus gland. Out of balance, it can cause serious maladies, including heart disease, high blood pressure, shallow breathing, and a variety of cancers (particularly breast cancer). The color associated with the heart chakra is green.

The fifth chakra is also known as the "throat chakra." Associated mostly with the spiritual body, it governs our mouth, throat, airways, lungs, and thyroid; and is connected intimately to our powers of expression. When in proper balance, it helps us communicate clearly, creatively, and tactfully with both the written and spoken word. It is also connected to feelings of inspiration, helping to promote artistic expression. When out of balance, however, it impedes our ability to express ourselves; we become cold, self-righteous, and insensitive. Physical ailments that can result from this state of affairs include asthma, hearing problems such as tinnitus, sore throat, and thyroid issues. The color associated with the fifth chakra is blue.

The sixth chakra is famously also referred to as the "third eye" chakra. It is connected to our intuition, perception, and understanding. When properly balanced, it fosters charisma, integrity, and clear-minded thinking. Alternatively, when out of whack it makes us feel scattered and often act inconsiderately towards others. Associated with the spiritual body, it governs our eyes, the base of the skull, and the pituitary gland. (The pineal gland is small, pine cone-shaped endocrine gland in our brains. It's responsible for producing melatonin, the hormone the affects our sleep patterns.) Not surprisingly, if our third eye chakra is out of balance, we can suffer from headaches, nightmares or hallucinations, vision and hearing problems, and sinus difficulties. The color associated with the sixth chakra is indigo.

The seventh and final chakra is known as the "crown chakra." Located at the top of head, it governs the upper skull, our central nervous system, the cerebral cortex, and the pineal gland. It is associated with the aspirations of the "higher self": idealism, reverence for life, spirituality. When in balance, it grants us a magnetic personality and a sense of peace; it empowers us toward sometimes almost miraculous achievements. When out of balance, however, it causes feelings of unwarranted superiority, a lack of concern about others, and a certain divorce from reality. Physically, if the crown chakra is imbalanced, it can lead to cognitive confusion, depression, and even severe mental illnesses like schizophrenia. It can also contribute to the onset or progression of diseases like Alzheimer's and Parkinson's. The color associated with the seventh chakra is violet.

There is no shortage of writing concerning the spiritual aspects of the chakra system, but that focus often leads to underestimating its impact on our whole health. Think of the chakra system as our "energetic body," complementing our "electrical" or nervous system. Its subtle frequencies can have a major impact on our physical, as well as our spiritual, well-being.

I had a patient who experienced not only a knot in her stomach, but an actual physical burning sensation in her upper abdomen before speaking in front of groups of people. Since her job required her to regularly address conferences and other large gatherings, it was a frequent and unwelcome — and sometimes almost incapacitating — problem.

While attending a meditation course, she heard about the chakra system and its impact. She began to suspect an energetic imbalance was the source of her stage fright, so she spoke to the instructor and received instructions on some basic breathing exercises, which she diligently performed.

To her surprise and relief, when she next stood before a crowd to deliver a speech, the pain she had previously felt was completely gone. In its place was a sense of peace and ease. As a result, her words and thoughts flowed better and more smoothly, and her level of performance increased dramatically.

Perhaps an even more dramatic example of the need to achieve a sustainable balance between our internal and external environments was another patient, who we'll call Leonard. Leonard came to me with severe lower back pain; chiropractic treatments gave him only a few hours of relief before it recurred.

During the treatments, Leonard began sharing some of the stresses he was under. His company had just been acquired by another firm, and there were rumors of significant job cuts on the horizon. He was convinced that his head was on the chopping block. He had a line on another opportunity, but it entailed a considerable pay cut. Should he take the sure thing, or gamble on an uncertain financial future?

Leonard's personal life was also filled with turmoil. His relationship with his long-term girlfriend had hit the rocks; it was clear that neither was happy, but ending the relationship also meant giving up a spacious rent-controlled apartment. If he lost his job — or even if he took the lower-paying one — he wasn't sure he could afford to maintain his standard of living.

Financial stress and feelings of being unsupported frequently manifest as lower back pain, so it seemed likely that these external pressures were causing his physical symptoms. But how to solve those problems?

I began by teaching Leonard some meditation techniques. He used them only infrequently at first, apologetically telling me that he was often too physically and mentally exhausted after work to remember to do so, and too anxious in the mornings to focus. Fortunately, however, a couple of his old college buddies convinced him to spend a long weekend with them at a mutual friend's lake house. Leonard took the opportunity to concentrate on his health: he meditated regularly, slept more soundly, got some fresh air and exercise, and shared plenty of laughs. Perhaps most importantly, he barely thought about his work problems or his relationship issues.

When I saw Leonard again a week or so later, I was amazed at the difference. He seemed so much more relaxed, both emotionally and physically. Trading his high-stress, overwhelmingly negative environment for a much more positive one was completely transformational for Leonard, even within such a short span of time. His internal condition reflected the quality of his external surroundings.

Of course, the challenge is attaining — and maintaining — that inner balance when we're not on vacation. It doesn't happen by accident, and sometimes it involves some difficult choices. But Leonard's example shows that to ignore the impact of our external environment places our health and happiness in jeopardy. We simply cannot compartmentalize our inner and outer selves; they are intimately, intrinsically, holistically connected.

Chapter Five

How Healthy Are You?

"The wish for healing has always been half of health."

-Lucius Annaeus Seneca, Roman philosopher

So what is health? We've spent the past several chapters coming to grips with this surprisingly elusive notion, seeing how different cultures and eras defined what it means to be "healthy." We've also explored just how far some of them were willing to go to achieve that goal, a theme that we see echoed in our own culture's obsession with achieving the "perfect body" or preserving our youth or "having it all" at work and home.

The fact is — and I take comfort in this — that these issues of health and happiness that we continually wrestle with are not unique to our generation or our society. We're simply the latest in a long, long line of human beings to wonder how we maximize the time we're allotted on this planet. Our questions about health are universal questions.

From my own studies, I've concluded that most universal questions either lack quantifiable answers altogether or have deceptively simple ones. That said, if we're going to make the leap from philosophy to practice we need a working definition of health specific enough to inform our decisions, but still robust enough to account for individual variances, changes over time, and unforeseen circumstances.

What does it mean to be healthy?

Before we arrive at a definition of what being healthy *is*, let's again specify what it *isn't*. Being healthy *doesn't* mean that you never catch a cold or get sick. It *doesn't* mean that everything in your body is functionally at 100 percent. It *doesn't* mean that you will, in middle age, suddenly become an Olympic-caliber athlete. It *doesn't* mean that you are always happy or fulfilled. And it *doesn't* mean that you're guaranteed to die peacefully in your sleep at the ripe old age of 103.

Keeping all that in mind, here's my definition of what it means to be healthy: *Health is the harmonious, balanced alignment of mind, body and spirit necessary to achieve and sustain each individual's optimal level of overall vitality and well-being.*

Let's dissect that just a bit further, so there's no confusion going forward. The key phrase is "harmonious, balanced alignment." What does that mean? Consider your car's engine. Whether you drive a Fiat or a Ford F-150, a Honda or a Hummer, virtually all contemporary internal combustion engine designs are simply refinements of a model invented way back in the 1870s by a German engineer named Nikolaus Otto. Otto's design used a piston housed inside a cylinder and connected to a crankshaft to power the engine. A cyclical process — intake, compression, power and exhaust — converts a fuel-air mix into the energy needed to keep the crankshaft moving. Because of these four steps, his design became known as a "4-stroke" engine.

Subsequent engineers found that adding more cylinders added more power, which is why most consumer vehicles now feature four-, six- or even eight-cylinder engines. But here's the thing: the cylinders have to fire sequentially, not all at once, or the engine won't be able to sustain continual power. If two of the cylinders are firing at the same time in a four-cylinder engine, for instance, you've lost a quarter of your overall power. As a result, the engine may stall or be difficult to start, or it may shake so badly that the vibrations can be felt in the steering wheel. Take a moment the next time you're idling at a traffic light to consider the intricate mechanical ballet going on under the hood.

Like a well-maintained four-stroke engine, good health is a result of our physical, mental, emotional and spiritual aspects all operating in concert, all in the proper balance and alignment with each other. When we talk about "firing on all cylinders," we mean that we're functioning smoothly, efficiently, and at a high level. There is no imbalance, no sense that career success (for instance) has had a prohibitive cost on our physical or emotional selves.

Unfortunately, like our car's engine, our health is generally something we take for granted . . . until the biological equivalent of our dashboard warning lights flare up. And sadly, even then we tend to treat our cars better than ourselves. Imagine driving along and suddenly seeing the "check engine" light wink on. Would you ignore it, figuring that it'll eventually go away? Or would you make an appointment with a mechanic to get it checked out ASAP?

Now think about your health. How many times have you experienced one of your body's "warning lights": insomnia, persistent migraines, feelings of irritability and agitation, panic attacks, chronic acid reflux? Did you stop and make your health a priority at that point? Or did you instead pop a pill (or two or three) and keep on going because you didn't think you had the time or money or ability to re-prioritize your life?

If so, just know that that's basically the equivalent of putting a piece of masking tape over the dashboard light; just because you can no longer see it doesn't change the fact that it's still on. Remember, the light itself isn't the problem. It's simply alerting you to the fact that there *is* a problem somewhere. Same with whatever symptoms you're experiencing — they're simply warning you that your mind, body and spirit are somehow out of alignment. It's your choice whether you attempt to mask the symptoms, or actually get to the root of the problem. Just know that, like a faulty engine, sooner or later you're heading for a burnout.

Notice too that our definition of health encompasses more than simply physical well-being. I hope the preceding chapters have helped make the case for the importance of our mental, emotional and spiritual states as well — again, something not only historically neglected in Western medicine, but increasingly even in Eastern medical tradition as countries like China and India become increasingly westernized. But the evidence for the tremendous impact of these non-physical spheres on our bodies is simply too overwhelming to ignore. Neglecting that aspect of our health is like committing to refilling your car with gas, but refusing to repair a short in the electrical system. Health — real health — is holistic.

Being healthy is being consciously aware of the choices we make on a daily basis. It's about how we make things authentic, real and balanced at work and at home, in our professional lives and in our personal relationships, in our vocations and our avocations. It's being attuned to our external and internal environments, so that when the inevitable rough patches arise, we are able to navigate them honestly, intentionally and correctly. Ultimately, being healthy is simply about being ourselves: our best selves.

With that said, just how healthy *are* you?

How healthy are you?

Chances are that you picked up this book because you're unsatisfied in some way with the quality of your life. Maybe it's a chronic physical ailment that has failed to respond to any treatment. Maybe it's a feeling of anxiety, depression or boredom that you just can't seem to shake. Maybe it's simply a nagging sense that the life you're living isn't really the life you wanted.

The first step is to assess where you are right now in your health journey. Below is a series of evaluative statements designed to help you determine an authentic level of functionality, health-wise. This assessment is not intended as the basis for comparing yourself to anyone else; your situation is as unique as you are. The purpose here is simply to help you take stock of your own life, right here, right now and establish a baseline for your current level of health.

I also want to include this caution: if you have reason to believe that you are in any imminent medical danger, please seek help from a licensed physician *immediately*. Do not wait, do not make excuses, and do not ignore your body's warnings— please, for your sake and the sake of those who care about you. Chapter Ten offers suggestions and tips for choosing a health care provider.

The assessment on the pages that follow is divided into four parts in order to allow you to evaluate your current levels of physical, mental, emotional and spiritual alignment. For each statement, you'll be asked to check "never," "seldom," "sometimes," "frequently" or "always." Each of those responses has a numerical value ranging from one to five. At the end of each section, you can total up your score to get a sense of how healthy you are in that area of your life. Add up the four section scores to see your overall holistic level of health and vitality.

Ready? Then turn the page to get started!

Section 1: Your Physical Well-Being	Never	Seldom	Sometimes	Frequently	Always
1. I sleep soundly and get a full night's sleep.	1	2	3	4	5
2. I wake up feeling rested.	1	2	3	4	5
3. I eat breakfast.	1	2	3	4	5
4. I have a regular morning and night time routine (stretching, movement, schedule).	1	2	3	4	5
5. My diet is composed of 70-75% fruits and vegetables.	1	2	3	4	5
6. I eat small amounts at regular intervals.	1	2	3	4	5
7. I take regular breaks throughout the day to move or clear my mind.	1	2	3	4	5
8. I drink at least 1.5 liters of water per day.	1	2	3	4	5
9. I exercise for at least 15 minutes a day.	1	2	3	4	5
10. I feel full of energy and vitality at least 75% of the time.	1	2	3	4	5

Section 1 Scores

Section 1 Total

Section 2: Your Mental Well-Being	Never	Seldom	Sometimes	Frequenly	Always
1. I feel positively mentally challenged/ motivated by my job.	1	2	3	4	5
2. I spend time reading about things I enjoy or find interesting.	1	2	3	4	5
3. I like learning new things.	1	2	3	4	5
4. I am able to concentrate and fully focus on the task at hand.	1	2	3	4	5
5. I cope with stress well.	1	2	3	4	5
6. I spend time engaged in my hobbies.	1	2	3	4	5
7. I feel mentally comfortable in my place of work.	1	2	3	4	5
8. My thoughts are positive ones throughout the day.	1	2	3	4	5
9. It's easy for me to organize and prioritize my daily activities.	1	2	3	4	5
10. I feel a sense of accomplishment at the end of most days.	1	2	3	4	5

Section 2 Scores

Section 2 Total

Section 3: Your Emotional Well-Being	Never	Seldom	Sometimes	Frequenly	Always
1. I have a positive outlook on life.	1	2	3	4	5
2. I feel at ease in my surroundings.	1	2	3	4	5
3. I am able to express myself honestly and openly to the people in my life.	1	2	3	4	5
4. I work with people who make me feel good about myself.	1	2	3	4	5
5. I have fulfilling relationships with healthy boundaries.	1	2	3	4	5
6. I am optimistic about the future.	1	2	3	4	5
7. I enjoy interacting with others.	1	2	3	4	5
8. I am able to use my gifts and talents throughout the day.	1	2	3	4	5
9. I smile often.	1	2	3	4	5
10. I believe I have the power to positively influence my health and well-being.	1	2	3	4	5

Section 3 Scores

Section 3 Total

Section 4: Your Spiritual Well-Being	Never	Seldom	Sometimes	Frequenly	Always
1. I meditate or pray.	1	2	3	4	5
2. I feel connected to others.	1	2	3	4	5
3. I sense a purpose for my life.	1	2	3	4	5
4. I practice yoga or meditation regularly, or I begin my day with a few minutes of reflection time.	1	2	3	4	5
5. I feel that I am a good person who positively contributes to others.	1	2	3	4	5
6. I am inspired by what I do for a living.	1	2	3	4	5
7. I practice gratitude everyday.	1	2	3	4	5
8. I read, listen to or watch inspirational books, music and/or videos.	1	2	3	4	5
9. I laugh a lot.	1	2	3	4	5
10. I spend time in nature daily.	1	2	3	4	5

Section 4 Scores

Section 4 Total

What does it mean?

So you've totaled up your section and overall scores, but before we talk about what they mean, let's briefly discuss what they *are* and *aren't* intended to be:

- They *are* intended to be an overall snapshot of your overall level of health.

- They *aren't* intended to be a tool for diagnosing individual diseases or dysfunctions.

- They *are* intended to help you assess the patterns of health in your life.

- They *aren't* intended to be a substitute for professional medical care.

- They *are* intended to be a general guide for reflecting on your habits.

- They *aren't* intended to be an absolute measure of your specific circumstances.

- They *are* intended to empower you to make healthy changes to your lifestyle.

- They *aren't* intended to discourage you from taking charge of your health.

With all that said, let's see how you did . . .

Section 1: Your Physical Well-Being

Tier 1: Reinforce (Score: 41-50). Congratulations! It's clear that you've made your physical health a priority in your life. You have regular routines in place to help you cultivate and sustain a high level of vitality. Keep on keeping on! To avoid the possibility of stagnation and boredom, you might consider adding to or changing various aspects of your routine.

Tier 2: Reevaluate (Score: 26-40). It's clear that you value your physical health and are practicing various activities to improve it. However, consistency might be an issue — perhaps you're finding it difficult to regularly find the time to devote to healthy routines. It might be time to reevaluate your lifestyle and make your physical well-being a more defined priority.

Tier 3: Reboot (Score: 10-25). Unfortunately, you've had a difficult time staying focused on your physical self. Perhaps you routinely elevate other aspects of your life — work is a common culprit — over your health. Perhaps you've neglected this area for so long that you're struggling to create healthy physical habits. Perhaps you feel selfish any time you think about carving out time for exercise or rest. Remember, though, that getting plenty of sleep, eating well and moving regularly are absolutely necessary for sustaining our physical selves. If your body isn't functioning well, everything else suffers correspondingly in your professional and personal lives. Investing in your physical health isn't selfish — it's simply wise. Now is the time to recharge your batteries, review your priorities, and readapt to a new reality. Begin slowly, adding a little a day or week at a time. I promise that by doing so you will gain the energy to accomplish your goals.

Section 2: Your Mental Well-Being

Tier 1: Reiterate (Score: 41-50). Your creative spark is lit, new ideas are flowing, and you are clearly open to change and learning in life.

You consistently feel mentally engaged and challenged. If there's any caution, it's that perhaps you are so engaged by the world around you that you sacrifice depth of knowledge for breadth of knowledge. Take some time and reiterate to yourself what new learning opportunities you really desire, then prioritize them.

Tier 2: Reassert (Score: 26-40). You likely don't feel consistently challenged; perhaps you are prone to falling into ruts in either your professional or personal life. You probably have moments of creative brilliance, but they often seem few and far between. Perhaps you are frustrated by an inability — perhaps as a result of your environment — to focus or concentrate for a sustained period. Perhaps you are not as open-minded and open to change as you once were. Now is the time to reassert your passion for what you *love* to do, not what you think you *have* to do.

Tier 3: Restore (Score: 10-25). You are stressed out and burned out, reactive instead of proactive. You might see yourself as a hamster running on a wheel: always moving, but never going anywhere. You need to take time to restore your mental strength by practicing your powers of concentration and creativity. It's vital that you pick something that will engage and challenge you.

Section 3: Your Emotional Well-Being

Tier 1: Refine (Score: 41-50). Your relationships with yourself and with others are healthy and balanced. Take some time to intentionally refine and further strengthen those essential relationships. You aren't afraid to express yourself in appropriate ways, but be sure that you cultivate an attitude of gratitude: receive as un-self consciously as you give to others.

Tier 2: Recalibrate (Score: 26-40). Some of your relationships are more balanced than others; perhaps things at work are great, but your personal life is considerably messier or less fulfilling. This is a direct reflection of the most important relationship in your life: your relationship with yourself. Take the time to recalibrate and nurture yourself. Delineate essential boundaries with others in order to balance the various aspects of your life. Spend time with friends with whom you aren't afraid to "be yourself."

Tier 3: Reclaim (Score: 10-25). You feel emotionally drained and/ or disconnected from those around you. Perhaps you feel that you consistently have to be someone that you're not, or that you must somehow live up to an impossible standard. Possibly, you're in one or more unhealthy, unsupportive relationships. This emotional stress has likely also taken a toll on your physical energy levels. It is vital that you reclaim your life and your right to be the person that *you* want to be.

Section 4: Your Spiritual Well-Being

Tier 1: Reflect (Score: 41-50). You feel connected to a larger purpose and to your true self, which sustains you through life's storms. Your spiritual practice is a high priority, one that you refuse to neglect. Reflecting upon the continued expansion of your consciousness and connection is food for the soul.

Tier 2: Reconnect (Score: 26-40). There are times when you feel like you can sense a bigger purpose in your life, but sometimes that clarity is crowded out by the mundane tasks of everyday life. To help you reconnect to that awareness more regularly, you might just need to work on some more consistent spiritual practices.

Tier 3: Rebirth (Score: 10-25). Your spiritual focus has become so myopic that it's difficult for you to imagine a world beyond the borders of your daily existence. You may feel a deep sense of discontent within even knowing why, even when you are materially and professionally well-off. Chances are you didn't always feel this way, so what you need is a spiritual rebirth. Start by getting back to nature.

If you scored at or near the Tier 1 level in all four categories, you are doing an excellent job of balancing and integrating all the aspects of health. Since there's always room for improvement where your vitality is concerned,

I'd recommend that you use the intermediate and advanced exercises in the chapters that follow in order to add some diversity to your existing health routines. You may also want to refer to the Resources section at the end of the book to deepen or extend your knowledge about various practices.

On the other hand, if your overall score is lower than you would like, don't panic or despair! The rest of this book is dedicated to helping you, no matter who are where you are, visualize and achieve positive change and measurable results in your health.

Where do we go from here?

I hope the preceding exercise has helped you take a hard, honest look at the current state of your physical, mental, emotional and spiritual health. Now comes the really exciting part: actually making the changes needed to move you to a happier, healthier, more fulfilled level.

The chapters that follow lay out specific changes you can make in each area to improve your overall level of health. Depending on your current level, that might seem daunting right now. The good news is that it's never too late to start. The not-so-good news is that it's going to take time. It's going to take effort. And most of all, it's going to take patience.

Chances are that the imbalances causing your health to suffer didn't develop overnight, but rather the result of years of bad habits and poor choices. Don't expect things to change for the better overnight, either. So be patient with the process — and most of all, be patient with yourself. Understand that each little change you make is a victory. Know that each little change you make brings you closer to your ultimate goal of a better, healthier, more authentically aligned lifestyle. Remember that each little change you make benefits not just you, but your family, friends, colleagues, company and community.

As the Chinese philosopher Lao Tzu once remarked, "The journey of a thousand miles begins with one step." Today is the day to take the first step on *your* journey to health. Today is the day to make a commitment to really living life, not simply enduring existence. Are you ready?

Chapter Six

Improving Your Physical Health

"If we could give every individual the right amount of
nourishment and exercise, not too little and not too much,
we would have found the safest way to health."

-Hippocrates

F ew, if any, American presidents have been as physically vigorous and adventurous as Theodore Roosevelt. In his mid-20s, abandoned politics to become a working cowboy in North Dakota. At 30, he resigned his post as Assistant Secretary of Navy after the U.S. declared war on Spain to personally recruit the first United States Voluntary Cavalry — the famous Rough Riders — and led the charge up Cattle Hill at San Juan, Puerto Rico.

After two terms as President, Teddy went on safari in Africa, came back to (unsuccessfully) challenge for a third term, then — in his 50s — led a grueling eight-month expedition into the jungles of South America to discover the source of one of the Amazon's major tributaries, the River of Doubt, which was subsequently renamed the Rio Roosevelt in his honor. When Roosevelt died in his sleep of a presumed heart attack in 1919, then vice-president Thomas Marshall commented, "Death had to take him sleeping. For if Roosevelt had been awake, there would have been a fight."

Given that impressive record of physical accomplishment, it might surprise you to learn that Teddy Roosevelt was the stereotypical 98-pound weakling growing up. As an infant, he developed chronic asthma, so severe that he often woke at night unable to draw breath. He was able to sleep only cradled upright in the arms of his father.

Roosevelt's asthma continued throughout his childhood. He also developed a variety of intestinal complaints and severe seasonal allergies. By the time he reached adolescence, he was a pale, short, painfully thin, narrow-chested youth with skinny legs. And that was when his father took him aside and said, "Theodore, you have the mind but you have not the body, and without the help of the body the mind cannot go as far as it should. I am giving you the tools, but it is up to you to make your body."

Teddy did not hesitate before responding: "I will make my body!" From that moment on, Roosevelt become a tireless champion of what he called the "strenuous life." His goal was to live each day to fullest, with vigor and vitality.

The tools his father spoke of were the contents of a private gym he had constructed in the family's New York house. There, under the patient direction of fitness instructors, Teddy lifted weights, did pull-ups, boxed, and pushed himself to exhaustion on the parallel bars. He became a voracious hiker and outdoorsman. As the months and years passed, the skinny, sickly teenager transformed himself into a muscular, broad-shouldered man.

Improving your physical level of health

Teddy Roosevelt's example should give all of us hope that no matter our level of physical health, it's always possible to improve it . . . even dramatically so. Consider another example, that of "the godfather of fitness," Jack LaLanne. Growing up in California in the early 1920s, he became, in his own words, "a junk food junkie."

"It made me weak and it made me mean," he recalled. "I had boils, pimples, and was near-sighted. Little girls used to beat me up."

By the time he was 15, he suffered to such an extent from headaches and bulimia that he was forced to drop out of school for six months. Desperate to help, his mother finally took him to hear a lecture about the benefits of good nutrition. Told by the speaker that he was a "human garbage can," Jack took the man's words to heart and vowed to change his life. He gave up sugar and meat, and devoted himself to lifting weights, swimming and wrestling. He became such a paragon of fitness that at age 54 he reportedly defeated then 21-year-old Arnold Schwarzenegger in an informal strength and body-building competition. "That Jack LaLanne's an animal," Schwarzenegger allegedly exclaimed afterward.

As with Teddy Roosevelt, LaLanne's transformation was the result of a complete shift of perspective. "You've got to train," he said. "You've got to eat right. You've got to exercise. Your health account, your bank account, they're the same thing. The more you put in, the more you can take out. Exercise is king and nutrition is queen: together, you have a kingdom."

You too can accomplish wonders with your physical health. It will take time. It will take effort. There will be days when you fall short, days when you feel discouraged, days when your goal seems far away. Accept that. Be patient with yourself. Give yourself permission to fail occasionally. Admit the frustrations that come with changing your life . . . and then pick yourself up and keep moving towards that goal.

Or to quote Theodore Roosevelt, a man who knew a thing or two about persistence, "It is only through labor and painful effort, by grim energy and resolute courage, that we move on to better things."

Beginning exercises

Climbers attempting to scale Mt. Everest don't race directly to the summit of its 29,029 feet. Instead they slowly, steadily make their way up to one of two base camps about 17,000 feet up the mountain's flank, stopping periodically to allow their bodies to acclimate to the increasing altitude. From base camp, they make a series of gradually more rigorous climbs, returning to base camp to rest and recover, before eventually attempting to summit the mountain. Weather and health permitting, the average expedition takes between four and six weeks.

The exercises below are your trek to the "base camp" of physical health. You may already practice some of these activities, although possibly sporadically. They are intended to help prepare you for the more strenuous exercises that lie ahead. Even if they seem a matter of common sense, I encourage you to treat each with a maximum degree of intentionality and focus. Doing so will help ensure maximum benefit, more quickly integrate healthy routines into your life, and prevent backsliding.

And no, you do not have to complete or "master" each of these before moving on to the next tier of activities. Listen to your body and proceed at the pace that seems best to you. Just remember: this is a marathon, not a sprint!

Walking

Movement is essential to good health. It's also a challenge in our increasingly sedentary culture. You can help reverse the trend by making walking a regular part of your routine. Start off slow and easy — 20 minutes a day is a great start

As you walk, be aware of your body's motion. Be mindful of your posture; hold your head up and your shoulders back and relaxed. Tighten your abdominal muscles and buttocks. Walk slowly at first to warm up, stopping to do some flexibility stretches. Then gradually increase your pace until you reach your target heart rate. You should not be gasping for air! Hydrate yourself before, during and after the activity, and be sure to end your walk with a cool down pace and a round of stretching to help prevent soreness and injury.

The most difficult aspect of any health program is making beneficial activity, whether exercise or healthy eating, a habit. Committing to 20 minutes a day for a minimum of five days a week is a good initial goal. If you can only start with 5 minutes a day of stretching because your schedule is too crowded, please do so. As that becomes easy for you, add five minutes to your daily walk for the following week. Keep adding time until you are reaching your desired goal, perhaps an hour of physical activity each day. Remember, though, not to exceed the point where it's still enjoyable for you — for a habit to be truly sustainable, it can't simply be a chore. Even if that means you can only set aside five or 10 minutes for physical activity, it's better than doing nothing.

Warm Baths

Warm baths — hydrotherapy — were a staple of Hippocratic medicine, and a proven method of relaxing the parasympathetic nervous system, which is the part of the autonomic nervous system responsible for activating the body's "tranquil" functions: stimulating the secretion of saliva or the stomach's digestive enzymes, for example. (The sympathetic nervous system, in contrast, helps prepare the body for action by increasing heart rate, releasing sugar from the liver into the bloodstream, and other "fight or flight" responses.)

To ensure that you're not activating the sympathetic nervous system, don't make the bath too hot. Optimally, your bath water should be only slightly warmer than your body temperature (about 37 degrees centigrade). Soak for 10-120 minutes to help detoxify and relax your muscles. For added benefit, add bath salts or essential oils: chamomile or lavender for relaxation, eucalyptus or rose for an energy boost.

Sleep

It's a fact that most of us simply don't get enough sleep. That's too bad, given how important sleep is to good health. A recent study presented to the European Society of Cardiology meeting found that men who had a sleep disorder were between 2 and 2.6 times more likely to have a heart attack and 1.5 to 4 times more likely to have a stroke over the 14-year period of the study. Another group of researchers from Columbia University found a connection between getting fewer than seven hours of sleep a night and high body mass index; other studies suggest that an inadequate amounts of sleep tricks the body into releasing more appetite-inducing hormones, leading in many cases to increased obesity.

The American Academy of Sleep Medicine, the largest physician-based organization for sleep medicine, recommends adults get between seven and nine hours of sleep nightly. To help ensure that you do so — and that your sleep is of the highest quality possible — consider these tips:

• *Establish a regular routine for going to bed and waking up.* It's tempting to stay up late and sleep in on weekends, but it's basically subjecting your body to the equivalent of jet lag. If you stick to a consistent schedule, chances are that your Monday mornings will be a lot more pleasant.

• *Keep your bedroom dark and cool.* Studies suggest that room temperatures between 60-67 degrees Fahrenheit are optimal for restful sleep. If setting the thermostat that low isn't practical, there are a number of bedding and mattress pad options that can help your body rid itself of excess heat.

• *Cut out caffeine.* Stimulants like caffeine affect everyone a little differently, but they tend to affect us more as we age. It also stays in our system longer than we sometimes think it does, so experts recommend laying off caffeine by early afternoon to ensure it doesn't negatively impact bedtime.

• *Avoid heavy meals and alcohol too close to bedtime.* Your body really isn't designed to digest food while you sleep, so a big meal too close to bedtime may actually keep you up at night. Protein is especially tough to digest, so if you do have to eat late, stick to lighter fare. Alcohol, meanwhile, may seemingly make it easier to drop off, but once your buzz wears off you're more likely to wake up frequently and sleep fitfully.

• *Turn off electronics at least an hour before going to sleep.* This may be the toughest guideline for busy Westerners to adhere to, but the science suggests it may be the single most effective. First, mental activity revs us up instead of helping us relax. Second, bright light — the kind emitted from television, laptop and smartphone screens — is one of the primary triggers to our brains that it's time to be awake and alert. Combine the two and it's no wonder that people complain about not being able to "turn their brains off." So do yourself a favor and power down well before bedtime. In fact, consider banning electronics from the bedroom altogether! And if you simply can't resist the siren call of the email chime, turn off the wifi altogether before turning in for the night . . .

Stretching

Stretching regularly improves joint and muscle flexibility, which in turn helps prevents injuries. It also promotes better posture, helping decrease back and neck pain. Beyond the purely physical benefits, it helps calm and clear the mind — a great way to start or end a busy day. And it doesn't take an inordinate commitment of time: even less than 10 minutes of stretching a day can still have a demonstrable positive effect on your overall level of physical vitality.

Here are a few stretches I've found to be especially beneficial:

- *Upper Back Release:* Start from a standing position, with your feet hip-distance apart. Keeping your arms straight, interlace your hands and round your upper back. Visualize your shoulder blades spreading wide as you hold the stretch for 2-3 deep breaths.

- *Standing Hamstring Stretch:* Start with your feet hip-distance apart. Using your hand as needed to balance yourself, bring your right leg up onto a step or bench. (As your flexibility increases, you can increase the height of the step.) As much as possible, keep your keep back leg straight and your front foot flexed. Don't round your spine. Take 4-6 deep breaths. Repeat on the other side. If you want to increase the stretch, hinge at the hips (not the waist or back), keeping your spine completely straight.

- *Outer Hip Stretch:* Using your hands to balance yourself, bend your left knee and lift your left leg onto the bed. Square your hips and make sure that the front knee is outside your front shoulder. Keeping your tailbone untucked and your spine straight, hinge forward at the hips, placing hands on the bed for support. Hold for 4-6 deep breaths, then change sides.

- *"The Hippie":* This one is courtesy of TV's Dr. Oz. Start from a standing position. Bend forward at the waist, until you can place your palms on the ground in front of you. Bend one knee and hold for 15 seconds, then change legs.

Hatha Yoga

Hatha Yoga refers to a set of physical exercises (known as *asanas* or postures) designed to align your skin, muscles and bones. Combined with meditation and conscious breathing exercises (known as *pranayama*), these postures also open the many channels (*nadis*) of the body — especially the main channel, the spine — so that the body's energy can flow freely. There are several different types of yoga, but since Hatha Yoga is easy to learn and foundational to each it makes a good starting point. Resources for beginners are listed in the Resources section at the end of this book, but a terrific starting place is *Hatha Yoga Illustrated*, by Martin Kirk and Brooke Boon. It's a valuable addition to any personal health library.

As a beginner, I recommend 20-30 minutes of Hatha Yoga two or three times a week. Find a quiet, dim space where you will be uninterrupted. Sit quietly and breathe deeply for a few moments before beginning. Begin the series slowly, maintaining your inward awareness throughout the various poses. Do not overdo the *asanas* or treat this as some sort of competitive activity.

If Hatha Yoga is still too physically strenuous for you at this point in your health journey, don't worry. You have another option: Iyengar Yoga. Developed over 60 years ago by master yogi B.K.S. Iyengar, it uses equipment like cushions, blankets, straps and blocks to help less flexible practitioners slowly move into the various *asanas*, hold each for a minute or so, and then rest for several breaths before moving on to the next pose. Its slow pace and use of assistive aids enable even the sick, elderly and disabled to practice. Iyengar Yoga is especially useful when recovering from injury.

A recent meta-analysis (a review of several scientific studies) by a group of Portuguese researchers even suggests that yoga offers significant quantitative benefits for those suffering from cardiovascular disease. The team found that patients who regularly practiced yoga improved their exercise capacity (peak VO2) by 22% and their quality-of-life (HRQOL) measure by 24% compared to those in the control group. "Yoga enhances peak VO2 and HRQOL in patients with (chronic heart failure) and could be considered for inclusion in cardiac rehabilitation programs," the research team concluded.

Other studies show that yoga can be an effective non-pharmaceutical treatment for chronic pain. At the 2015 annual meeting of the American Pain Society, Dr. Catherine Bushnell, scientific director for the Division of Intramural Research at the National Center for Complementary and Integrative Health, explained how mind-body techniques such as yoga and meditation can have a measurable physiological effect. "Practicing yoga has the opposite effect on the brain as does chronic pain," said Bushnell. "Insula gray matter size correlates with pain tolerance, and increases in insula gray matter can result from ongoing yoga practice. The encouraging news for people with chronic pain is mind-body practices seem to exert a protective effect on brain gray matter that counteracts the neuroanatomical effects of chronic pain."

Intermediate exercises

After you feel comfortable with the basic exercises described above, you're ready to expand your physical health horizons by adding a new set of activities:

Conscious Eating

A friend of mine is a notorious "tapper." Many times I've been with him, listening to a lecture or watching a movie, when I hear the persistent "tap-tap-tap" of his pen or, in the absence of a prop, his finger. He is always vaguely apologetic, even a little embarrassed, when I point it out — the fact is that he's not even aware he's doing it.

How often do we bring that same unconscious mindset to our food? Have you ever unknowingly consumed a whole bag of chips while watching TV? Ever been so engaged in conversation that you didn't realize you'd wolfed down an oversized plateful of food? Ever snacked on something without even being particularly hungry, just because you "needed" something to do with your hands?

Conscious eating (sometimes also called "mindful eating") is about being fully engaged during meals, savoring each bite, being absolutely intentional about what we're putting into our bodies. It's a proven method for weight loss and healthy eating, but more than that it's a practice for looking at the world through a more focused lens, for being truly aware of every facet of our existence.

I encourage you to give it a try. First step: never, ever eat in front of the television or computer screen. Mealtimes must be inviolate so you can give your food your full and undivided attention. Take the time to reflect on how you feel when eating. When do you truly feel full? What emotions do you experience while eating certain types of food? How do you feel afterward? If possible, keep a written log or diary so you can more easily identify patterns . . . and hold yourself accountable.

Although it may feel a little strange initially to approach your food with such single-minded precision, it will help you eliminate overeating and recognize how certain foods affect your mood and energy levels. In time, you'll learn how to systematically fine-tune your diet for maximum benefit.

Steam

"Taking a steam" may evoke images of sweaty, towel-clad men in a schvitz or sauna, but the fact is that you can take advantage of the health benefits of steam without leaving your own home or investing in expensive equipment.

Inhalation therapy is a well-established treatment, dating back to the ancient Egyptians, for respiratory ailments like cold, flu, sore throat, bronchitis, sinusitis, asthma and allergies. Inhaling steam moistens dry air passages and acts as a natural expectorate by loosening mucus and relaxing the muscles of the throat and chest, thereby alleviating painful coughing. The warm air also helps dilate your blood vessels, promoting blood flow throughout your body. The increased circulation can be particularly beneficial in offering relief from headaches and migraines.

To take advantage of steam therapy without a gym membership, boil a few cups of filtered water and then pour it into a large bowl. Place a towel over your head and lean over the bowl. Breathe deeply through the nose for 10-15 minutes. Remember, the water is very hot, so take care to avoid burns.

Steam therapy can be enhanced by adding two or three drops of various essential oils to the bowl. Some of the most popular and effective treatments include:

- Peppermint or eucalyptus for sinus congestion
- Chamomile or lavender for headaches
- Chamomile, lavender or lemongrass for overall relaxation

Qi Gong

Often referred to as "Chinese yoga," Qi Gong ("chee-*kung*") is a 5,000-year-old health method that combines slow graceful movements with mental concentration and breathing to increase and balance a person's vital energy. "Qi," sometimes written "chi," is usually translated to mean the life force or vital energy that flows through all things in the universe, while "Gong" refers to a skill that is cultivated through steady practice.

The gentle, rhythmic movements of Qi Gong help reduce stress, build stamina, increase vitality and enhance the immune system. Several studies have shown that regular practice of Qi Gong techniques can demonstrably improve your cardiovascular, respiratory, circulatory, lymphatic and digestive functions. Devoted practitioners of Qi Gong often say that it helps restore vitality and speed recovery from illness.

One advantage of Qi Gong is that, because it does not rely on sudden movements or hard impacts, it is accessible to virtually anyone, at any age or level of health. There are a number of excellent resources available, some of which are listed in the Resources section at the end of this book. The most important thing, however, is choosing the right instructor. In selecting one, be sure to consider their background and level of experience, their attitude and their ability to meet you and teach you on your level. The Qi Gong Institute (www.qigonginstitute.org) maintains an online directory of reputable instructors by country and state; I highly recommend it as a starting point in your search.

Advanced exercises

If you've spent a few months or more diligently focusing on this aspect of your health, utilizing some or all of the tools described in the previous two sections, odds are that you're ready for the activities described below. A constant theme in this book has been the inter-related nature of health; that is especially evident once we reach this level. If you feel like you're not seeing the benefits you expected at this point, it's likely that you need to broaden your focus to include one or more of the other three areas — mental, emotional and spiritual — as well. Remember, you simply cannot be fully physically healthy if you have significant deficits in any of those other aspects.

Nutrition

Like many of these exercises and activities, we could write a whole book — or even a library — just on nutrition. Turn on the news or open your browser and the odds are good that you'll see some nutrition-related story. Particularly in the West, we're obsessed with food. Every year, it seems like some new fad diet sweeps the nation: the Mediterranean Diet, the Atkins' Diet, the South Beach Diet, the Paleo Diet, the Raw Diet. Unfortunately, since the weight loss industry is big business, these diets tend to be represented as life-changing panaceas rather than means to an end.

Worse, their advice (and the "scientific" claims on which it's based) is often wildly inconsistent and even contradictory. *Coffee and red wine are bad for you. Wait, they're good for you! Some carbs are good. Wait, all carbs are bad!* It's enough to make any non-dietician's head spin.

So what we're concerned with here is not advocating any particular "system," but simply encouraging you to empower yourself by taking charge of what you put into your body. If you've been practicing conscious eating, you've likely discovered the power certain foods have over your sense of physical well-being and vitality. Now it's time to take it up a notch.

We make poor food choices for a variety of reasons, chief among them time constraints and habit. If you want to truly focus on nutrition, you have to practice what we might call "conscious shopping." Instead of grabbing what's quick, take the time to shop carefully and intentionally. Educate yourself about ingredients, genetically modified organisms (GMOs) and production methods. This takes time and effort — it's entirely possible that we're talking about changing your whole lifestyle, after all — but the reward for doing so can be incalculable.

In general, your goal is to seek out healthier food choices and preparation options. It goes without saying that you should avoid processed foods and deep-frying. But you should also as rule adjust your diet until seasonable fruits and vegetables comprise 70-75% of what you eat. Whenever possible, I also advocate eating only locally-grown produce to ensure a healthy balance of vitamins — too often, commercially-grown fruits and vegetables are not grown in rich soil, and so don't absorb the optimal amount of the requisite nutrients.

Aromatherapy

Aromatherapy is a perfect example of a long-established therapeutic treatment finally getting its due from modern science. A number of recent clinical studies have found that the biochemical composition of various essential oils, many of which have been used for centuries, really does stimulate a measurable response from the body at a molecular level. They are as marvelously complex as any synthetic drug, but completely natural.

Beyond the purely physical effects, the use of aromatherapy also positively impacts our emotional and spiritual health as well. According to Dominique Baudoux, founder of the industry-leading scientific and medical aromatherapy laboratory Pranarôm (http://www.pranarom.com/), fragrances can powerfully stimulate the more primitive parts of our brains, eliciting an emotional response. Essential oils also bio-electrically stimulate the body's vibrational state, enhancing the effects of various energy therapies you might be using. Baudoux says that no other substance, natural or synthetic, can boast this same kind of triple benefit.

As a result of this tremendous versatility, aromatherapy can be used to treat a wide range of issues, including circulatory disorders, gastroenterological disturbances, dermatological issues, arthritis, gynecological problems, nervous disorders, cardiological concerns, even diseases. In short, as Badoux points out, there isn't a single area in which essential oils couldn't be used to provide relief and healing, either in combination with — or in many cases, instead of— "traditional" synthetic pharmaceuticals.

A few words of caution from Dominique Baudoux, who is a pharmacist as well as an aromatologist: in a very few cases, the use of an essential oil may interfere with the action of synthetic drugs. This is especially true in the case of anticoagulants. In general, though, the natural and the synthetic can coexist without a problem. More important is that any essential oils you use are 100% pure and natural. Buy essential oils only from trusted companies that either produce the oils themselves or deal directly with the actual producer. For instance, Pranarôm is extremely careful to control the supply chain of its products, which are currently sold in more than 10,000 stores worldwide. Baudoux's philosophy is that the more middlemen that are involved, the greater the risk of fraud. He advises consumers to make sure all aromatherapy products considered for purchase are certified by gas chromatography and mass spectrometry (GC-MS) to ensure they are chemically pure.

Tibetan Rites

The Tibetan rites refer to a yoga routine based on a ritual of exercises discovered in the early 1900s, but dating back to a much, much earlier era. Performed regularly and correctly, they can have a rejuvenating effect on the body. The rites are composed of five different movements, with each movement performed up to 21 times. It is best to start with three repetitions of each exercise and gradually increase the repetitions. The entire routine can usually be completed in less than 10 minutes.

As you'll remember from Chapter Four, our bodies have seven principal energy centers, or chakras. These rites stimulate the chakras, helping promote energy flow from your core to your extremities. One positive effect of this action is that it helps correct hormonal imbalances, which medical research suggests may lay at the heart of the aging process. By normalizing our hormone levels, we preserve youth, health and vitality.

I've included brief descriptions and illustrations of the five Tibetan Rites on the following pages. For more detailed information, refer to the Resources section at the of the book.

Rite One: Spinning

Rite One (Spinning):

The first rite is the practice of spinning. As one spins clockwise, the body's energy system is stimulated and negative energy is flung out.

Stand erect with arms extended from your shoulders with the palms facing down. To help prevent dizziness, focus your vision on a single point straight ahead as you begin to spin. At each revolution, as quickly as possible refocus on that reference point. Stop spinning as soon as you feel slightly dizzy. Lie on the floor and breathe deeply before you begin the next rite. Gradually increase the number of spins up to 21.

Rite Two: Leg Raise

Rite Two (Leg Raises):
The second rite is similar to familiar abdominal exercises. It is designed to create an extra stimulus to the solar plexus chakra.

Lie flat on your back on a thick rug or yoga mat. Fully extend your arms along your sides and place the palms of your hands against the floor. Then, raise your head off the floor, tucking your chin against your chest. As you do this, breathe in deeply and lift your legs, knees straight, into a vertical position. If possible, extend your legs back over the body, toward the head, but don't bend your knees. Then breathe out and slowly lower both your head and legs — again, keeping your knees straight — to the floor and relax your muscles. Repeat.

Rite Three: Camel

Rite Three (Camel):

The third rite opens the solar plexus and heart chakras, helping increase our sense of harmony and increase our overall energy level.

Begin by kneeling on the floor, knees under your hips. Keep your toes flat and your body erect. Place your hands on back of your legs, just under the buttocks. Tilt your head forward and tuck your chin against your chest. Then tilt your head and neck back, arching your spine backward. Inhale deeply and look upward. Exhale as you return to the original position. Repeat up to 21 times, breathing rhythmically.

Rite Four: Tabletop

Rite Four (Tabletop):

The fourth rite stimulates the sacral chakra, as well as strengthening and toning the legs and glutes.

Sit on the floor with your legs extended. Your feet should be flexed and about 12 inches apart, your palms flat on the floor next to your hips. Tuck your chin against your chest. Now tilt your head backward as far as it will go. At the same time, bend your knees and push up to a "tabletop" position, keeping your arms straight as you breathe in deeply. (Your body should be in a straight line with the upper portion of your legs, horizontal to the floor.) Tense every muscle in the body, then relax them and breathe out as you return to your original sitting position. Continue breathing in the same rhythm while you rest between repetitions.

Rite Five: Up Dog and Down Dog

Rite Five (Up Dog and Down Dog):

The final rite powerfully invigorates the energy currents of the entire body, increasingly your overall sense of strength and well-being. It is the most powerful of the five Tibetan Rites, as it requires your body to move in concert, moving energy up the spine.

Begin on all fours with your toes flexed and your palms on the floor. Your weight should be distributed evenly among your knees, palms and the balls of your feet. Start with your arms perpendicular to the floor and your spine arched downward, so that the body is in a sagging position. Keeping your hands and feet straight, slowly lift your buttocks toward the sky. Flatten your back and lower your head so that your body makes an inverted "V." Tuck your chin to your chest. Pause, then lower your buttocks until your legs are in a plank position parallel to the ground, with your chest out and shoulders back. Inhale on the way up; exhale on the way down. Repeat up to 21 times.

Martial Arts (Tai Chi)

It may seem a bit incongruous to mention martial arts here, but rest assured that I'm not suggesting you sign up for an MMA cage match. Believe it or not, certain martial arts — especially tai chi — utilize a variety of physical movements and forms that promote body awareness and overall fitness. And you never have to throw a punch or make a roundhouse kick!

In fact, in recent years tai chi has become very popular as a means of reducing stress and increasing body control. It involves a series of slow, gentle movements that flow from one formalized posture into the next. Tai chi has often been described as "meditation in motion."

An increasing focus on the health benefits of regular tai chi practice has revealed a whole host of potential benefits, including decreased levels of stress and anxiety, increased energy and stamina, increased flexibility, strength and balance, increased aerobic capacity, improved quality of sleep, and decreased blood pressure and cholesterol levels. It may also provide an overall boost to the body's immune system.

There are five styles of tai chi, all but one named after its founder. Each takes a different approach to the movements of the various forms, having been developed for a different purpose. Within each style there are still more variations, or schools. That said, there are far more similarities between the styles than there are differences. All use slow-motion, flowing, circular movements to promote balance and strength. All develop your chi. Most importantly, all provide important health benefits.

Choosing the right style for your needs is largely a matter of personal preference. The most popular one is the Yang style; it tends to be what most people visualize when they hear the words "tai chi." The second most popular style is the Wu style, which tends to emphasize smaller, more compact movements than the Yang style. Together, with dozens of variants between them, the Yang and Wu styles make up more than 80 percent of tai chi practitioners.

Chen style is actually the oldest form of tai chi, but accounts for only about one percent of practitioners these days. It alternates slow motion movements with short, explosive ones. As a result, it requires more coordination and is more physically demanding than the other styles, making it less than ideal for beginners or anyone not already in good physical health.

Hao style is very rare even in China. Considered an advanced style, it focuses primarily on internal chi movements. As a result, its physical motions tend to be extremely small-frame and nuanced movements.

Finally, so-called combination styles have become increasingly popular in recent years, mixing and matching movements from the other four tai chi styles as well as borrowing from other martial arts such as *bagua* and *hsing-i*. The intrinsic variability within this style makes it ideal for finding a school suited to your individual tastes. Unfortunately, that same variability often makes it difficult to know just want you're getting yourself into. This is definitely a case where taking the time to do a little extra research will likely pay a sizable dividend.

Final thoughts

Our physical health is only a part of a greater whole, but it's a vitally important part. It can have profound effect on our mental, emotional and spiritual states, for good or ill. As you focus on this aspect of your overall health, you're also establishing a solid foundation. And a final word of advice: enjoy yourself. It matters more than you may realize.

Susie came into my office complaining of general back pain. She was in her mid 50s: divorced with three kids, stressed out by issues of time and money. A nurse, she also frequently worked long shifts that were physically, mentally and emotionally draining. She admitted to feeling burned out — she felt that between her job and her role as a single mom, she was always taking care of others and never able to find any time for herself. Over the past couple of years, her weight had increased — fast food was both convenient and inexpensive — as had the number of sleepless nights. The back pain was the final straw.

Susie had also fallen into a self-destructive cycle: every few months she would throw out the junk food and throw herself into a new diet (she'd tried them all, or so it seemed) and exercise routine. She would lose a few pounds . . . and then plateau. The excess weight stubbornly refused to come off, the workouts became increasingly more difficult to fit into her crazy schedule, and she craved — and occasionally binged — on the foods she'd been stringently denying herself. A month or so into her new fitness regimen, she'd completely fallen off the wagon. The more this cycle repeated itself, the more Susie's self-esteem eroded.

As we dissected every aspect of her lifestyle, it became clear that there was one common denominator in her repeated failures to affect positive change in her health. She hated all of it. The dieting, the exercise — they were just more chores to add to an already overburdened list. It was no surprise that she found excuses to sabotage her efforts; frankly, I was impressed that she had the fortitude to go back to the fitness well time after time.

It was clear, though, that we had to change her perception of what it took to be healthy. So instead of recommending that she sign up for spin classes or another round of Krav Maga, I asked her what physical activities she enjoyed doing. It turns out that she liked walking, but she worried that it wasn't vigorous enough to qualify as a workout. On my recommendation, however, she committed to making that the focal point of her fitness regimen. I also encouraged her to start eating consciously rather than attempt to suddenly overhaul her entire diet. Finally, I recommended that she establish a regular nighttime routine.

Susie was astonished by the results. Suddenly, health became a way of life for her rather than a goal or destination. When I saw her six weeks later, she had not only lost some of those stubborn pounds, but her energy level had increased dramatically . . . as had her frame of mind. She was sleeping more soundly and enjoying her job again, and her back pain had mostly subsided.

I kept tabs on Susie as the months passed. Gradually, she expanded her repertoire of healthy activities. Walking became jogging, conscious eating became an increased attention to buying fresh and local. She even took cooking classes to learn how to maximize the taste and nutritional value of what she was buying!

Susie was successful because she was able to make positive changes and stick to them. I know that you can do the same!

Chapter Seven

Improving Your Mental Health

"It is only in sorrow bad weather masters us;
in joy we face the storm and defy it."

-Amelia Barr, 19th century British novelist

The good news is that mental health receives far more attention and far less stigmatization today than it did even 20 years ago. Both medical professionals and the general public are much more aware of the importance of good mental health, and much less prone to attach judgment where it's concerned. In fact, according to the U.S. Department of Health and Human Services, estimated expenditures for mental health reached $239 billion, up from $121 billion in 2003 and $42 billion in 1986.

The not-so-good news is that mental health spending is growing at rate a *slower* than spending on other health issues, again according to the USDHHS. Moreover, most of that growth is in prescription medicines, particular those designed to treat depression, anxiety and attention-deficit disorder. In short, we've become very adept at alleviating the symptoms associated with mental dysfunction, but less so at treating the underlying conditions.

I think part of the difficulty is that we still underestimate how much this aspect of health impacts and is intertwined with all the other areas, which leads to misdiagnosis and mistreatment. Consider the case of Lisa.

Lisa came to see me at age 35. Outwardly, she seemed a positive and gracious person with an infectious laugh. She was experiencing pain in her lower back and along her diaphragm and a feeling of tightness in her abdomen. And she was worried.

At age 24, Lisa had been in a terrible accident. She was hospitalized for months. At the time, doctors doubted she would ever walk again unassisted. As a gymnast and aspiring fitness instructor, the prognosis was a devastating one for Lisa.

Fortunately, she refused to give up on herself. Supported by a rehab doctor who shared her optimism, she began using positive visualizations during her extensive physical therapy. Within two years, she was not only able to once again walk, but actually participate in sports. Doctors, nurses and therapists who knew her case called a "medical miracle." Lisa felt she had been given a second chance at life.

And yet, here she was almost a dozen years after the accident, worried that her recovery was somehow illusory, that her second chance was about to be taken away.

And here's where her story gets really interesting . . .

After examining her, I determined that she had a few vertebral subluxations at her atlas and in her lumbar spine, which I treated using chiropractic techniques. But that alone didn't really account for her other symptoms. I suspected at least some of the abdominal issues might be related to food allergies, so I recommended she be tested. As it turns out, that was right on the mark — she was allergic to several of the foods she regularly ingested. But it didn't deal with the more serious back and diaphragm pain, symptoms that Lisa was becoming more and more convinced were somehow a relapse of her horrific injuries of nearly a decade ago.

The more I interacted with her, the more I sensed that her bubbly persona was really just a facade — a mask covering deep pain and insecurity. Eventually our bond of trust grew to the point where she admitted as much to me. Suddenly the picture came into focus.

As she opened up, it became clear that her lengthy recovery process had given her a mission in life, a purpose. Once it was truly over, she felt rootless and anxious. She had a nagging, constant fear that something bad was about to happen. Instead of dealing with that feeling, she repressed it beneath a veneer of forced optimism, expecting — hoping — that it would go away on its own. But unfortunately for Lisa, it didn't. In fact, it slowly grew worse as time passed.

Now that we had uncovered the real issue, we began to treat it with a daily regimen of meditation and yoga. She had never tried either, but was an interested and eager student. Over time, she became quite adept at both. More importantly, she also regained her positive outlook on life . . . and as she did, her physical pain diminished and eventually disappeared. Her optimism, once forced, became an external manifestation of genuine inner peace and joy.

Finding mental balance

Lisa did not have, according to either the traditional or even most contemporary definitions, a mental illness. What she had is more accurately termed a mental "imbalance." But consider how powerful the mind is, that this mental imbalance psychosomatically significantly impacted her physical self, causing real pain and discomfort. Ignoring the real cause of her problems simply exacerbated the symptoms. If she had been given antidepressant or anti-anxiety medication, it would not have remedied the root cause of that imbalance.

Back in Chapter Three, we explored the mind-body connection and the almost unbelievable power of our subconscious minds. We saw how past traumas or unhealthy patterns of thinking can, sometimes years later, have a profound impact on our overall state of health. If we can learn how to harness that power, however, we can use it to positively affect our health. In fact, Lisa had intuitively done just that after her accident, when she used positive visualization techniques to aid the healing process. What her doctors saw as miraculous was really just more evidence for the tremendous power of the mind.

Whether you have a major imbalance that needs correcting or just need a mental "tune-up," the exercises listed below can help. As with the previous chapter, please remember that these do not occur in a vacuum. All four aspects of health — mental, physical, emotional and spiritual — are intertwined and interdependent. If you neglect even one of those areas, you could end up undermining the other three aspects, with potentially disastrous consequences.

Beginning exercises

Just like with physical exercise, mastering the techniques below takes time, patience and practice. Start slow and build your mental stamina gradually.

Affirmations

Louise Hay and Wayne Dyer have long asserted the value and power of daily affirmations in exorcising negative mental energy and eliminating "deficit thinking." In his book, *Excuses Begone*, Dr. Dyer lists 18 common excuses we use when facing challenges ("I can't afford it") and the positive affirmation we can use to defeat that particular piece of negativity ("I am connected to an unlimited source of abundance"). His book is a great place to start, but there's no shortage of other resources.

Whether you use pre-made resources or choose to create your own, here are a few tips for getting the most out of affirmations:

- *Make them personal.* Your affirmations should focus on *your* goals, expectations and behavior. Unless you feel connected to what you're saying, the power of the affirmation will be dramatically reduced.

- *Make them positive.* You'd think that this goes without saying, but I've seen plenty of affirmations that were intrinsically counterproductive because they drew the practitioner's attention to a problem, not a goal.

- *Make them simple.* Back in the 90s, it was all the rage for companies to have mission and vision statements. Executive teams would spend sometimes dozens of man-hours (or more) trying to get the wording just right. And what happened when they were finally finished? Generally, not much. The statements were usually so convoluted from trying to shoehorn in every last goal that employees couldn't remember them, much less articulate them. Don't make the same mistake with your affirmations. Keep them short, simple and authentic.

- *Root them in the present.* Affirmations are really about creating an alternate reality for yourself, not about wishing for a better future. They're designed to positively impact our attitudes and behavior right now (which will help in the achievement of the goal we set for ourselves) rather than lapsing into a kind of hopeful procrastination (which doesn't change anything). So phrase accordingly: "I *am* poised and confident" rather than "I *will be* poised and confident." Remember, words (and thoughts) have the power to affect the universe.

- *Repeat them often.* Like the mission/vision statement example, an affirmation that isn't used is a waste of time. Speak your affirmations often to yourself throughout the day: when you get up, while you shave, driving to work, during your lunch break, etc. Or record them and listen to them while in the car. Some people even prefer to write them out a dozen or so times two or three times a day. Experiment to find which approach works most powerfully for you.

Inspirational Readings

There is a rich tradition in many of the world's religions concerning oral reading or recitation of prayers, hymns, scriptures, etc. Just the act of saying these inspirational, comforting words out loud can help re-align your mental processes and give you a new perspective on your reality. In the words of Louise Hay, "I believe we create our own lives. And we create it by our thinking, feeling patterns in our belief system. I think we're all born with this huge canvas in front of us and the paintbrushes and the paint, and we choose what to put on this canvas."

If religious readings are not your thing, other inspirational readings will also work. These can range from poetry to positive stories to quote-a-day calendars. Quantity is not as important as quality.

Set aside a few minutes for your reading. I recommend doing it the first thing in the morning, before the day begins making demands on your time and attention. Find a solitary place for your reading; if the weather is favorable, a patio or balcony is especially ideal. Whatever you do, do NOT turn on your computer, tablet, smartphone or television. Make a commitment to be fully present during this time.

Read the selection once through silently. Then read it aloud. Reflect on the words, the phrasing, the meaning, the feelings or memories the passage evokes. Sit for a few moments absorbing the power of the passage; time permitting, read the part(s) that you most connected with a final time.

This regular ritual creates a sanctuary for you in the midst of even the most trying times. It allows you to pause and gain perspective before jumping into the chaos of daily life — and it's amazing how often you'll find yourself drawing comfort and strength from those words you read during the day that follows.

Sleep

Our mental state is profoundly affected by our sleep patterns. According to a 2005 "Sleep in America" poll, people who were diagnosed with depression or chronic anxiety were more likely to sleep less than six hours at night. In a 2007 study of 10,000 people, those with insomnia were five times as likely to develop depression as those who slept normally. Worse, depression and insomnia can be mutually reinforcing, setting up a particularly nasty feedback loop in which the less sleep you get, the more depressed you become, and the more depressed you become, the harder it is to fall asleep. On the positive side, treating sleep problems can also help alleviate feelings of depression and anxiety (and vice versa).

Lack of sleep also negatively affects our memory and judgment, even when we think we're doing fine. "Studies show that over time, people who are getting six hours of sleep, instead of seven or eight, begin to feel that they've adapted to that sleep deprivation — they've gotten used to it," says sleep expert Dr. Phil Gehrman. "But if you look at how they actually do on tests of mental alertness and performance, they continue to go downhill. So there's a point in sleep deprivation when we lose touch with how impaired we are."

For specific tips on how to maximize your sleep, refer to Chapter Six.

Intermediate exercises

In practicing the exercises listed in the previous section, hopefully we've already begun to notice some positive effects. Now you're ready to start using some more rigorous, disciplined techniques. As before, be open to new strategies and patient as you learn how to apply them.

Meditation

As we discussed in Chapter Three, we are often not even consciously aware of how our own minds can sabotage our well-being. Neuroscientists refer to a "negativity bias," a tendency to focus more on negative experiences than life-affirming ones. The theory is that this negativity bias was originally a survival instinct, a valuable evolutionary trait that prompted our Paleolithic ancestors to pay more attention to avoiding potential threats like the sabretooth tiger nearby than focusing on more positive attributes like the beauty of a Stone Age sunrise. While it's hard to argue with efficacy of this mental conditioning in that particular eat-or-be-eaten environment, unfortunately for us it also means that our brains are wired to focus primarily on negative experiences. That in turn means that we tend to get stuck in mental feedback loops of anxiety, depression and futility.

Meditation is a time-proven method for breaking that mental cycle of negativity and replacing it with a consciously positive mindset. A study conducted by Massachusetts General Hospital found that even a couple of months of regular meditation actually produced physiological changes to the brain, including growth in areas associated with stress regulation, empathy, sense of self and empathy. Another study out of UCLA found that meditation helped participants with attention deficit disorder (ADD) tune out distractions and focus better. There are few — if any — better tools for helping us achieve calm and clarity in the midst of life's external and internal storms.

There are a multitude of meditation practices to choose from, including well-known ones like transcendental meditation and Zen. I find that it's usually easiest to begin with primordial sound meditation (PSM), a technique developed by Dr. Deepak Chopra and Dr. David Simon. PSM is uses a mantra, a vibrational sound created by the universe at the time and place of your birth. Calculated using ancient Vedic mathematical formulas, the mantra you use is intensely personal and unique.

Silently repeating your personal mantra shifts your awareness from the analytical, intellectual side of your brain, gradually allowing you to enter a deeper level of awareness. PSM is usually practiced sitting down, with a focus on comfort.

If using a mantra feels strange — as it often does for beginners — I often suggest simply sitting or lying down on a yoga mat and using meditation music specifically developed to balance your brain waves and help you achieve a calm, relaxed state of mind as you focus on slow, rhythmic breathing. The challenge for many patients is learning not to fall asleep in this setting! If that's an issue for you, try lighting a candle and spending a few minutes simply staring at the flame, focusing in on its movements and colors.

If you're really struggling to "empty" your mind during meditation, you might consider "active meditation." It uses simple repetitive physical tasks to hone your focus. For instance, you could practice active meditation while walking, taking the time to consciously notice each step. If you can do this barefoot, to increase the sensation of the ground's texture, so much the better.

Intentional visualization
Intentional visualization has gained both popularity and legitimacy in re-

cent years, surprisingly because of its increased use by professional athletes. A handful of studies in the field of sports psychology have suggested that athletes who intentionally visualized on-field activities like hitting a major league pitch or smashing a tennis serve experienced the same results as those who actually physically practiced those tasks. As a result, intentional visualization has become more prevalent especially during periods of rehabilitation from injury, as athletes seek to minimize the atrophying of their skills.

Even if you're not an athlete, intentional visualization can be a powerful tool. Think about a future situation or desire. Then focus in detail on the sensations you would feel, the sounds you would hear, even the scents you would hear or flavors you would taste. Stimulating all your senses positively anchors the feeling and enhances the power of the visualization.

Visualization is all about intentionality. Be strategic about what you choose to visualize and why, then mentally create this reality as vividly as possible. Repeat often. Doing so engages your subconscious mind, which can't differentiate between a detailed visualization and a "real" event — it registers what you're visualizing as though it's really happening. That in turn reinforces positive thoughts and elevates your entire state of mind.

Advanced exercises

Affirmations, meditation and visualization provide a solid foundation from which to begin practicing more advanced mental exercises like those listed below. Even more than the previous section's techniques, these require sustained focus. The goal is to make them habitual. So practice, practice, practice!

Vision boarding

Vision boarding is one of my favorite activities. Simply put, a vision board is a tool used to help you identify, clarify and concentrate on a life goal. Think of it as taking intentional visualization to the next level.

A vision board is a poster board or a digital equivalent on which you place images (or even words or phrases) relating to that goal. You can use your vision board during your daily affirmations to help keep you focused amid the distractions of the daily grind. It powerfully stimulates both the conscious and subconscious mind by reminding you visually of where you want to be or what you want to accomplish. Here's how to do it:

- *Block out some time in your schedule.* You can do this solo or with a friend, especially if you share a common goal.

- *Pick a color.* Select a colored poster board that resonates to you. The actual color doesn't matter; what does is that you feel good when looking at it.

- *Pick a theme.* Are you trying to visualize your dream vacation? Maybe a loving relationship? If you can't winnow it down to one theme, consider making multiple vision boards. On the other hand, if you're visualizing your desired life, you certainly can include diverse images that representing the different facets of that reality. Just be clear and intentional about what it is that you're visualizing!

- *Select images.* Collect a few magazines and look through them to find pictures that summon the feelings or goals you want to attract into your life. Then clip them and paste them on the board. If you don't have magazines, you can also search the internet and print out appropriate images.

- *Put a photo of yourself at the center of the board.* You can also include motivational quotes or inspiration words or phrases.

Keep your vision board free-flowing, but still with at least a semblance of organization. You want a board that helps you focus on your goal, not one that distracts you from it because of its chaotic cluttering of images.

Place the board in a spot where you can see it every day. Regularly update it, removing older images and adding newer ones to keep it fresh. You may even find it beneficial to go through the entire process from scratch on a regular basis. I recommend creating a vision board at the beginning of a new year, when we tend to be focused on goals and resolutions, and again about midyear, when we often need to give ourselves an accountability check about how the year is progressing.

Refer to the Resources section in the back of this book for more information on setting up and using your vision board.

Mindfulness

In the last chapter, we talked about "conscious eating" as a means of avoiding over-eating. That strategy is really just a subset of the overall concept of "mindfulness." *Psychology Today* describes mindfulness as "a state of active, open attention on the present." So often we're so consumed by worry about the future or regret about the past that we become essentially a spectator to the present, allowing our lives to slip past without really being aware.

Buddhist sages call this the "monkey mind," in which we veer from thought to thought like monkeys swinging from tree to tree. Perhaps you've experienced this on your commute — so consumed with thoughts about what tasks you needed to accomplish that day that you ended up driving on "autopilot," snapping out of it only to realize that you'd arrived at your destination. Or maybe you lie awake at night, unable to "turn off your brain" as you replay the events of the day just passed or obsess about what's on the docket for tomorrow.

"Ordinary thoughts course through our mind like a deafening waterfall," writes Jon Kabat-Zinn, the biomedical scientist helped pioneer the use of meditation in mainstream medicine. To restore balance to our lives, we have to learn to control our thoughts instead of being controlled by them. We have to learn how to, in Kabat-Zinn's words, "rest in stillness, to stop *doing* and focus on just *being*."

Mindfulness involves creating a nonjudgmental awareness of the present: becoming a more detached and careful observer of your thoughts, instead of allowing them to knock you around like a barrel going over Niagara Falls. By doing so, you gain he ability to more fully experience life as it happens.

The health benefits of mindfulness are many: stress reduction, lowered blood pressure, lower risk of heart disease, a healthier immune system, increased happiness and contentment, a reduction in impulsive behaviors, improved attention, and less conflict with family, friends and coworkers.

Here are some tips for cultivating mindfulness no matter your lifestyle:

- *"Check in" with yourself frequently.* Take a number of short breaks throughout the day to practice being present. If you have trouble remembering to make the time, set an alarm to remind you. During these check-ins, focus on taking slow, regular breaths. Reflect on any sensations within your body that you are experiencing at that moment.

- *Practice being an observer of your own thoughts.* Especially when in the midst of a high-stress, try to focus inwards. Ask yourself, "Am I distracted right now? What is my self-talk at this moment?" These types of questions, asked and answered, will help develop a habit of consistent mindfulness.

- *Take advantage of downtime.* When taking your morning shower, consciously take the time to feel the sensation of the water cascading down your body instead of planning out your first meeting of the morning. When commuting to the office, force yourself to be aware of the vehicles, people and scenery around you instead of mentally composing an email.

Final thoughts

"Every thought we think is creating our future," wrote Louise Hay in a profound testament to the power and scope of the human mind. As we've seen, our minds can dramatically affect our physical and emotional well-being, so we simply cannot afford to neglect this aspect of our health.

One example of this power was 16-year-old Maggie, who came to my office after falling off her horse. She had been riding competitively since the age of seven, so her skill and experience were not the issue. But lately she'd had more than her share of falls. Her father thought it might be a problem with her balance — perhaps something like vertigo — but after a slew of tests, her medical doctors ruled out any physiological cause. One suggested attention-deficit disorder as a possible cause, but her parents balked at that idea, and especially at the prospect of side effect-inducing ADD medication.

Maggie's father was a long-standing patient of mine, so he decided to bring her in so I could determine if the fall had caused any major vertebral subluxations in her back. Besides, he reasoned, perhaps there was some undetected spinal issue that was affecting her overall function and causing her recent troubles.

My first impression of Maggie was of a bright, vivacious, fairly typical teenager. She had always been a good student (although her father told me her grades had also recently declined a bit), she had plenty of friends, and she was active in cheerleading and sports. As Maggie and I spoke, though, she admitted that she was also intermittently experiencing insomnia and an inability to concentrate.

I asked her about her horseback riding — specifically what was different about it compared to a few years ago. After a little bit of resistance, she finally admitted that balancing her riding practice schedule with the academic pressures of high school were beginning to take a toll on her. She said she wondered, often while riding, what her friends were doing . . . and what she might be missing out on as a result of her rigorous practice schedule. That said, she couldn't bear to give up riding outright!

So basically we had a very normal, very conflicted teenaged girl who didn't know exactly what she wanted or what to do. The problem was that her mental distraction could result in serious physical harm if she continued to mistime jumps. A bad fall could potentially result in paralysis or even death.

To help Maggie learn to focus her mind, I suggested that she begin practicing active meditation during warm-ups and cool-downs, and even while brushing her horse. Rather than allow her mind to anxiously wander to thoughts of her social life, I encouraged her to use visualization techniques to stay positive and remain fully present in the moment.

Maggie was very receptive to my suggestions (to my relief) and began to experience almost immediate improvement. Not only did the mysterious falls stop, but so did the insomnia. Even her grades bounced back!

The techniques I taught Maggie were so successful that she was able to continue riding regularly through the remainder of high school, all through university (from which she graduated with honors), and even through the demands of law school. Today she continues to serve as a part-time riding instructor in addition to her full-time law practice. She has become such an advocate for the use of visualization that she actually teaches the fundamentals to her beginning students to help them overcome their fears and more quickly connect to their horses. She tells them candidly that her ability to focus, visualize and be present in every aspect of her life has been the greatest driver of her success, both professionally and personally.

As with physical exercise, the mental exercises we've just explored take time and effort to master. In the words of the philosopher Aristotle, "We are what we repeatedly do. Excellence then, is not an act, but a habit."

This is more than simply creating a positive habit, though. This is about engineering a whole new *lifestyle* for yourself, one that is healthier, happier and more fulfilling. This is about changing your future for the better. Don't wait! As the old saying goes, today is the first day of the rest of your life — make the most of it!

Chapter Eight

Improving Your Emotional Health

*"It is only in sorrow bad weather masters us;
in joy we face the storm and defy it."*

-Amelia Barr, 19th century British novelist

To me, he will always be Cha-Cha Charlie. I met Charlie when he was 87 years young. He came in complaining of headaches and fatigue, but he seemed in excellent shape. In fact, I was so sure that I had misheard his age that I asked him to repeat it — honestly, I had mistaken him for 20 years younger. Despite the outward appearance of health, though, it soon became evident that he was in genuine distress, plagued by almost nightly headaches that prevented him from sleeping soundly.

Trying to find the root cause of his pain, I asked him about his diet, his activity level, his water consumption, and several other physical health indicators. All seemed near optimal, especially for a gentleman approaching nine decades on the planet.

Something that soon became apparent, though, was how flat and detached Charlie was. He seemed completely passionless. In the course of our conversations, he mentioned that his wife had passed away four years previously, but declined to provide any more details. He did tell me about the trip they took to India to celebrate their 50th wedding anniversary, and given my own Indian heritage we had a great conversation about various aspects of Indian culture, including healing practices, yoga and spirituality.

Unfortunately, his physical symptoms failed to improve after a couple of sessions. I did notice that his hips and pelvis seemed more flexible, however, and given the holistic nature of health I thought it might be significant. Jokingly, I mentioned that his hips were moving so well that we should get him on the dance floor.

To my shock, he began crying uncontrollably.

Weeping, shuddering, he tried to apologize. He literally could not stop the tears. I encouraged him to just let it all out; it was painfully clear that he had been holding back a lot of emotional turmoil. Finally, with the help of a glass of water and some deep-breathing exercises, he was able to calm himself.

Then Charlie told me the reason for his breakdown. Dancing had been a passion for him and his late wife. They had begun dancing socially, but eventually took classes and became good enough to participate in a couple dozen competitions. It was as they were preparing to leave for one of those competitions that his wife suffered a massive heart attack, dying almost instantly.

As Charlie spoke, his sense of loss and grief over her death were palpable. At his core, he simply had been unable to move on from that pivotal moment. I gently suggested that he consider taking up dance again, that doing so might help him keep her memory alive in a more emotionally healthy way, that it might re-energize and re-invigorate him. And perhaps, just perhaps, it would alleviate his headaches and general feelings of lethargy.

When I saw Charlie again a few weeks later, he told me that he had decided to follow my advice and re-enroll in dance lessons. And then an amazing thing happened.

As he began to truly emotionally heal, Charlie's physical symptoms gradually abated. His headaches disappeared. He began sleeping soundly again. His overall energy dramatically improved. In short, he rediscovered his passion for life.

A couple of years later, I was privileged to see Cha-Cha Charlie win a seniors dance competition; he continued dancing — and living life to the fullest — until his death at age 95. It was a phenomenal illustration of the power our emotional selves have to affect our mental and physical states.

Focusing on your emotional health

For all the recent media attention on mental health, emotional health still generally gets short shrift from society at large. Particularly here in the West, there's a prevailing attitude of "just get over it" that hampers us from taking the time and effort to focus on our emotional well-being. Too often we suppress the healthy expression of our feelings because we are fearful of appearing publicly weak or flighty or unstable. But as Charlie's example demonstrates, avoidance isn't a treatment. Sooner or later, the consequences of neglecting our emotional health manifest themselves in the other areas of our lives, as physical dysfunction, mental impairment or spiritual distress. Perhaps no other aspect of health is as closely intertwined with the others.

Consider bullying. In recent years, bullying prevention programs have become a major focus of American schools as educators and policy-makers responded to a series of dramatic and high profile news stories about students taking their own lives after being physically and emotionally harassed by peers. In the wake of those tragedies, teachers began explicitly focusing on fostering empathy for others. Doing so has produced some surprising revelations.

"Most of us have assumed that the kind of academic learning that goes on in school has little or nothing to do with one's emotions or social environment," writes researcher Joseph Zinns. "Now neuroscience is telling us exactly the opposite. The emotional centers of the brain are intricately interwoven with the neocortical areas involved in cognitive learning."

Put simply, how we *feel* directly impacts how well we *learn*. Despite this, a recent *EdWeek* survey of American teachers, school administrators, and instructional specialists found that fewer than half of the respondents felt the majority of their school's students possessed "strong emotional and social skills." Without that skill set, potentially millions of children are at greater risk of a whole litany of physical, mental and spiritual problems, including headaches, gastrointestinal pain, respiratory difficulties, insomnia, high blood pressure, back/neck pain, a weakened immune system, and a greatly increased chance of alcohol and drug addiction.

American society is gradually — but slowly — changing its opinion towards emotional health, but the old attitudes are sometimes deeply entrenched in our culture. The image of the strong, self-sufficient "man's man" who rarely expresses emotion and *never* discusses his feelings . . . well, let's just say that it's still very much in evidence. When Green Bay Packers quarterback Brett Favre tearfully broke down in 2003 after winning a game the day after his father died, there was no shortage of snide comments of the "real men don't cry" variety to counterbalance more sympathetic, laudatory ones.

The bottom line is that we have a long way to go until our culture values emotional well-being at the same level that it does physical health. Mental health issues, which are often deeply and integrally connected with emotional dysfunction, are still regularly, and even systematically, stigmatized. We are collectively uneasy in airing our emotional laundry. If you don't believe me, the next time a colleague or acquaintance greets you with "How are you?" give them an honest and extended answer — and watch how quickly most people will attempt to disengage from the conversation!

Beginning exercises

Because our emotional self is so thoroughly integrated with the other facets of our health, it is essential that you build a firm foundation at the outset. Believe that you have the right to be happy. Never waiver in that belief, and never surrender power over your emotional well-being to anyone or anything else; never fall into the trap of thinking that the acquisition of additional material possessions will affect permanent change.

Surround yourself with positivity

"You are the average of the five people you spend the most time with," according to author and entrepreneur Jim Rohn. Ask yourself: *Who are the people in my life I can really "be myself" around? Who are the ones who leave me feeling energized? Who are the ones I instinctively turn to in times of success and sorrow?*

Now look for some common denominators. Make a list of characteristics that describe those individuals and define those relationships. Those are the attributes that support your emotional health, the values that add energy to your emotional stockpile instead of taking from it.

Use this list to begin evaluating the people with whom you regularly spend time and the activities you share. How well are you all aligned? Do you leave a lunch meeting or a dinner party completely drained? Do you find yourself almost subconsciously finding excuses to avoid seeing certain "friends," relatives, coworkers, or acquaintances? Those are signs that you probably should reconsider the frequency and duration of your associations with those folks.

What do you do if a disproportionate number of those negative people inhabit your workplace? Frankly, it might be time to take a hard, honest look at your choice of company or career and weigh it against the importance of your health. Decide where your priorities really lie.

But if it's simply not feasible for you to make those kinds of sweeping professional changes at this point in time, it's even more vital that you intentionally surround yourself with positive and uplifting folks outside of work. What activities energize you? What hobbies get you excited? What kinds of service opportunities fulfill you? Find like-minded people and spend time cultivating those relationships. They very well may be our lifeline to a healthier emotional state.

Give yourself permission to say "no"

Often we compromise our emotional health through over-committing. We usually have the best of intentions, but the cumulative effect of over-extending ourselves can take a dramatic toll, particularly on our emotional health. One of the most transformational skills you can develop is to give yourself license to say no.

When asked to do something, consider how well it aligns with your core values. Does the prospect make you feel excited or resentful? If it's the latter, the healthier (and more honest) response is simply to decline. Don't feel the need to tell a little white lie; be non-confrontational but truthful. Chances are that your honesty will actually increase the other person's regard for you. They may be disappointed, but they'll likely respect your candor.

If time is the issue, perhaps you modify your "no" into a "not right now." I've passed on many intriguing offers and opportunities simply because I thought my plate was already too full. Some came back around when circumstances were more favorable; others didn't. That's okay, too. I've learned to trust my gut about what's worth taking on and what I should take a pass on — you can, too.

Indulge your creativity

Because the day-to-day demands of work and family can undeniably take an emotional toll, it's vital that you find some outlet to rejuvenate yourself. Perhaps it's an intellectual activity like writing or painting, or a service activity like Habitat for Humanity, or even a physical activity like hiking or kayaking. Whatever it is, make it a priority. Too often we feel guilty about making time for these activities when there's still work to be done or chores that need attention. The reality, though, is that there will *always* be more work and more chores. You can never entirely stem that tide, and spending all your time focused on doing so leads only to ever-diminishing returns.

One of the core tenets of emergency management is that first responders must take steps to secure their own safety when entering a hazardous situation. It's not a question of courage or a desire for self-preservation; the rationale is that if the responders become incapacitated themselves, no one will be able to provide the same level of assistance to victims. In effect, they become part of the problem rather than part of the solution.

While the mundanities of daily life pale in comparison to the adrenaline-fueled efforts of firefighters, police officers, and paramedics, the self-care philosophy is still valid. If you are emotionally exhausted, you will be far less effective both personally and professionally. You will be less creative and more prone to mistakes, miscommunications, and conflict.

Taking the time to replenish your creativity isn't being selfish. It's a necessary investment in becoming the most productive person possible.

Intermediate exercises

Once you've done some basic work on your emotional foundation, you're ready to move on to some more specific exercises designed to improve your emotional health. As always, keep in mind that your emotional well-being is intricately connected to your physical, mental, and spiritual states as well. Don't neglect one for the sake of another!

Vision-boarding

We talked in the last chapter about the practice of vision-boarding, which is a fantastic way to help you specifically identify your goals. I love vision-boarding, not least because it's such a creative process. We'll talk more about the Law of Attraction and other Universal Laws in the next chapter, but the précis is that like tends to gravitate to like. This has been unfortunately much abused as some sort of get-rich-quick gimmick, which it definitely isn't.

What the Law of Attraction really articulates is that we attract the circumstances on which we are focused and with which we are emotionally in vibrational harmony. Chances are you know someone who seems to be a magnet for drama and dysfunction. Their Facebook updates are constantly filled with tales of Springer-esque woe, to the point that you wonder how so much can happen to one person. Wonder no more — that's just the Law of Attraction at work.

When we create a vision board, we're consciously reframing our focus, which in turn changes the kinds of events, people, and circumstances we draw to ourselves. We begin to think about what's possible with anticipation, rather than dreading the unknown. By doing so, we create what is in effect a positive feedback loop, with potentially amazing results.

If you're unsure about embarking on vision-boarding solo, the good news is that you don't have to. Find a friend open to trying it alongside you. There are also vision-boarding workshops offered in many communities, which offer the added benefit of the opportunity to connect with like-minded people embarking on a similar journey.

Practice forgiveness

All of us carry emotional scars inflicted, sometimes purposefully, sometimes unknowingly, by others. Often it's those closest to us that wound us the deepest. But without condoning the actions that caused such pain, without conceding anyone's right to misuse you or treat you badly, I submit to you that refusing to forgive hurts you more than the perpetrator. That's not metaphorical; it's physiological. When a memory is evoked, your subconscious automatically summons the same physiological response you felt initially. We literally experience the event all over again, which means dwelling on a past hurt only perpetuates it.

In 1984, Jude Whyte lost his mother to the sectarian violence rampant throughout Northern Ireland when a bomb exploded outside her Belfast sitting room. The device was placed on her windowsill by the Ulster Volunteer Force, a Protestant terrorist organization locked in a life-or-death struggle for the future of Northern Ireland with the Catholic-led Irish Liberation Army. Like many Irish Catholics, Jude's anger was directed at the UVF as well as the police who were widely seen as collaborators.

"In those days there was no counseling or trauma advice and initially I was full of bile and hatred," Jude remembers. "I was a bad father, a bad husband and a bad (teacher). My thoughts were only of revenge and I could feel the bitterness eating me up. Eventually I had a nervous breakdown and knew I had to change."

Did it help?

"Forgiveness was for me both a pragmatic decision and an emotional feeling," Jude says. "It meant that I lived a lot easier, I slept a lot better. You could say my revenge for the murder of my mother is my forgiveness because it has given me strength. I don't forgive on behalf of my mother but for the pain that was inflicted on me for the loss of my mother."

One exercise I've found that has helped me forgive is by taking the time to write an actual letter to the person describing how their act made me feel. I've even used this exercise towards people who have died — the point is not to *send* the letter, but to *write* the letter. This writing therapy is wonderfully cathartic, wonderfully liberating.

Dr. James Pennebaker, a professor in the Department of Psychology at The University of Texas at Austin, has conducted a number of research studies on the therapeutic value of writing. His findings show that short-term focused writing can help people dealing with a wide range of emotional traumas ranging from terminal illnesses to divorce to job difficulties to the effects of violent crime.

"When people are given the opportunity to write about emotional upheavals, they often experience improved health," Pennebaker says. "They go to the doctor less. They have changes in immune function. If they are first-year college students, their grades tend to go up. People will tell us months afterward that it's been a very beneficial experience for them."

Pennebaker's research confirms that the value resides in the act of writing itself; even if the writing is immediately destroyed, the therapeutic benefit remains unaffected. Basically, our minds are designed to try to make sense of events. When an event is traumatic, they go into overdrive attempting to process the experience; if you've ever lain awake at night thinking about the same thing, over and over, you know exactly what I mean.

Pennebaker found that writing helps make an experience more understandable to our own brain.

"Emotional upheavals touch every part of our lives," Pennebaker explains. "You don't just lose a job, you don't just get divorced. These things affect all aspects of who we are: our financial situation, our relationships with others, our views of ourselves, our issues of life and death. Writing helps us focus and organize the experience."

As a result, we not only sleep better, but may also find our memory and ability to concentrate improve . . . as do the quality (and perhaps even the quantity) of our social interactions.

Advanced exercises

By this point you've hopefully cleaned out a lot of your emotional baggage and are ready to cultivate some healthy and sustainable emotional habits. Celebrate your progress and continuing charting a positive course!

Keep a gratitude journal

Especially if you tried the writing therapy exercise described in the previous section and found it helpful, I encourage you to consider keeping a gratitude journal. The practice is deceptively simple — and deceptively powerful.

Any time you feel emotionally drained or in turmoil, it's difficult to summon positive feelings on demand. That's what makes this an "advanced" exercise for most people. It requires a level of discipline that you may not be ready to take on earlier in your journey. To keep a gratitude journal, you basically commit to carrying around a small notebook and jot down anything you encounter throughout your day that elicits feelings of gratitude. Perhaps it's someone holding a door open for you, or paying you a compliment, or allowing you to merge into traffic. Perhaps it's the feeling of the warm sun on your face, or a cool breeze ruffling your hair. Perhaps it's a hug from your child, or the affections of a pet.

If it's not feasible for you to keep a running list throughout the day, you can also take a few minutes before bedtime to reflect on the day's events and make your list. It doesn't matter if the list seems repetitive — what's key is sincerity of feeling. If you are truly grateful for the items you write down, your subconscious will buoy your mood and improve your resilience.

Meditation

We also discussed meditation previously, so I encourage you to read that section in Chapter Seven as well as consult the list of resources at the end of the book. Meditation is a time-proven method that benefits all four areas of health: physical, mental, emotional and spiritual.

If your specific concern is your emotional well-being, however, it is important that you pay particular attention to your breathing techniques. Breathing from your diaphragm will stimulate the lower lobes of your lungs and activate your parasympathetic nervous system, which will in turn help calm anxiety you may be feeling. Achieving this kind of breath control requires concentration and practice, but it is well worth the effort.

Certain breathing patterns can also help activate the chakra system we discussed in Chapter Four, facilitating the flow of positive energy throughout your body. When we focus on this system, we activate the neuroemotional centers that allow us to access more energy. Engage all of your chakras and your ability to respond to stressful situations calmly — rather than react emotionally — is heightened tremendously.

A few years ago, several San Francisco middle and high schools instituted a stress-reduction meditation strategy called "Quiet Time." One of the earliest Quiet Time adopters was Visitacion Valley Middle School, a campus afflicted by high rates of truancy, student violence, poor academic achievement and (unsurprisingly) staff turnover. The school had tried all sorts of strategies ranging from after-school tutorials to peer counseling programs to sports, but nothing seemed to work . . . until Quiet Time, that is.

The results of this period of campus-wide meditation were nothing short of astonishing. The number of disciplinary suspensions fell by almost 50% the first year, and within four years was among the lowest in the city. Daily attendance rates climbed to 98%, well above the average. Grade point averages also increased dramatically, as did staff retention rates.

Visitacion Valley's success has prompted other area schools to institute similar Quiet Time meditation times. They also have experienced significant decreases in both student and staff incidences of stress, conflict, anxiety, ADHD and depression; and increases in self-esteem, academic achievement, retention and creativity.

B.E.S.T.

Developed by Dr. M.T. Morter, past president of Logan College of Chiropractic and The Parker College of Chiropractic, the Bio-Energetic Synchronization Technique (B.E.S.T.) is a hands-on energy balancing procedure that helps reestablish your body's full healing potential by eliminating the interference created by our conscious minds.

There are both physical and emotional versions of B.E.S.T. The physical version utilizes light pressure on specific points on the body's surface to address parasympathetic and sympathetic imbalances, which often manifest as both acute pain and chronic conditions. A trained practitioner holds pressure points along the patient's spine, sacrum and skull, providing relief from spinal muscle spasms and nerve pressure.

Emotional B.E.S.T. helps identify negative thought patterns caused by emotions like worry, guilt, fear, and judgment. Left untreated, those patterns interfere with the body's natural healing abilities. In this technique, practitioners work with patients to "rewrite" those patterns, many of which are caused by past traumas. Freeing the mind from the limiting effects of those negative memories allows it to fully exist in the present, and optimizes its amazing natural resiliency.

Final thoughts

In my practice, one of the toughest challenges I face is treating patients with deep emotional hurts. It's also one of the most rewarding. And never has that been truer than in the case of Keith.

To all outward appearances, Keith was a well-groomed, well-dressed, well-spoken professional, a high tech entrepreneur who was smart and funny. He came in complaining of frequent tension headaches. Curiously, they affected him as much or more during weekends and vacations as during the workweek. He also suffered from frequent bouts of insomnia.

I sensed that there was more to the story during the intake session, however. I asked Keith some fairly standard questions: "Do you feel happy?" "Do you feel stressed?" "Have you experienced a sense of loss?" It was if a wall went up. Keith suddenly looked like someone who would rather be anywhere else but in my exam room; for a moment, I literally thought he was going to bolt out of the office altogether.

I quickly moved on to my examination, and gradually Keith seemed to relax. I treated his physical symptoms and wondered if he would come back.

He did, despite the fact that despite my efforts there was little improvement in his condition. I intuitively sensed that there was more to his dysfunction, that the root cause was not physical at all. I began using a bioenergetics technique designed to address whatever emotional "program" was running in the subconscious.

Ten minutes into the treatment, Keith's emotional dam burst, and I was deluged by a flood of tears. For several minutes he wept, crying so hard at times that he was literally gasping for air. I comforted him as best I could and waited for the turbulence to subside.

When it did, I learned the reason for his earlier emotional distance. Two years previously, his wife had committed suicide while he'd been away at a conference. She had struggled for years with extreme social anxiety and depression, but Keith thought she'd been doing better. Her death took him completely by surprise, and left him struggling to care for their two young children while coping with the shock of her death. He blamed himself for not seeing warning signs, for devoting so much of his time and attention to his growing business instead of his family, and most of all for not being there that fateful weekend.

He admitted that this had been the first time he'd allowed himself to actually shed tears over her death. At home he felt he had to appear strong for his children, that he had to stay upbeat and in control. But now it was like all that grief and guilt rushed in, as fresh and powerful as they'd been immediately after his wife's suicide.

I advised Keith not to fight those feelings, even though they were painful. Rather, he should accept them, be present in them, and focus on forgiving both himself and his wife. I suggested he take the rest of the day off and — for a change — put his emotional well-being first.

He agreed and followed my advice. Two days later, he was back in my office asking for another of the bioenergetics treatments. As emotionally painful as it had been, he felt like it actually had helped alleviate some of his physical symptoms, that somehow the two were connected (which, of course, they absolutely were).

After a month of intensive treatment, Keith's physical difficulties were almost gone. Just as important, he admitted that he was beginning to "feel" again. I gave him some additional suggestions for activities that might help his emotional healing, and he eagerly accepted.

Keith remains one of my more memorable patients, but his case — while dramatic — isn't unique. We all bear emotional scars. We all tend to build walls around our feelings. We all want to pretend that everything is just fine. For a while, we may even fool ourselves into believing it really is. But sooner or later, reality intrudes, and unless we address the underlying emotional issues involved, we can never truly find healing and happiness.

Chapter Nine

Improving Your Spiritual Health

*"The new physics provides a modern version of
ancient spirituality. In a universe made out of energy,
everything is entangled; everything is one."*

-Bruce Lipton, biologist and author

They're called the "eight-thousanders": the 14 mountain peaks higher than eight thousand meters above sea level. At that elevation, the so-called "Death Zone," the human body simply can't survive very long. The lack of oxygen, the frigid cold, the exposure to gale-force winds, the treacherous footing, and a myriad of other challenges make summiting even one of the eight-thousanders a noteworthy achievement in the tight-knit, highly competitive climbing community. But the highest accolades are reserved for the handful of climbers who have succeeded in summiting all 14 eight-thousanders: 33 of them, as of this writing. Less than three dozen souls out of the seven billion people living on the planet. No question that's some pretty elite company.

And then there's John Gill. Gill is legendary even among members of the eight-thousand club, a climber whose technical skills have vaulted him onto lists of the all-time greats: Sir Edmund Hillary, Reinhold Messner, Hermann Buhl, and Royal Robbins.

Here's the truly stunning fact: *John Gill has achieved this exalted status entirely as a result of ascents less than 10 meters high.* That's right — Gill doesn't climb mountains, he climbs boulders.

According to author Jon Krakauer:

Make no mistake: Gill's ascents may be diminutive, but by

no stretch of the imagination are they easy. The boulders he climbs tend to be overhanging and lacking in fissures or rugosities substantial enough for lesser climbers to even see, let alone stand on or cling to. In effect, Gill's climbs distill the cumulative challenges of an entire mountain into a compact chunk of granite or sandstone the size of a garbage truck or a modest suburban house. It is no exaggeration to say that the summit of Mt. Everest could sooner be reached by most climbers than could the summit of any one of a score of Gill's boulders.

So what motivates someone like John Gill to not only eschew the standards of success that define his sport, but to completely invert them? "The boulderer is concerned with form almost as much as with success," he says. "Bouldering isn't really a sport. It's a climbing activity with metaphysical, mystical, and philosophical overtones."

Whereas most climbers define success by whether or not they reach the summit of a mountain, Gill doesn't even regard summits as particularly important. "The more obscure the pattern, the more difficult the appearance of the rock, the greater the satisfaction," Gill says. "There is something there that can be created, possibly, if one uses insight an intuition to make this quantum jump. One discovers that a bouldering route can be accomplished not by looking at each minute hold, foot by foot, but by looking at the overall problem. The reward . . . is almost continual enlightenment."

When Gill began to focus on boulders rather than peaks, of course, he was derided more than admired. Many of his fellow climbers simply assumed he'd lost his nerve for being at high altitude. In reality, he was pursuing an inner path that combined physical exertion with spiritual enlightenment. "I wasn't interested in making my climbing fall into a category, walking in someone else's footsteps, or obeying a set of . . . rules, even if unwritten rules," Gill remembers.

Interestingly, Gill is a longtime student of Zen, who uses meditation to, as Krakauer writes, "clear his mind, prime his body, and give him the calm assurance necessary to get him over sketchy terrain."

"(There are) times when I feel as though I'm being sewn into the rock," Gill says. "I can come closest to this second reality, this feeling of lightness. And that, really, is the transcendental poetry of climbing. I consider experiencing that hypnogogic state to be far more important than being able to climb extremely difficult boulder problems that nobody has climbed."

Discovering spirituality

In recent years, it's become increasingly common for everyone from evangelical preachers to self-styled motivational gurus to reference "mountain-top experiences": emotionally-charged, spiritually-transformative events. It's no secret that many mega-churches invest in state-of-the-art visual effects, professional caliber music and carefully crafted inspirational sermons in an attempt to create a regular Sunday morning mountaintop experience for participants. They have discerned — correctly, I think — that people are hungry to connect with something outside themselves.

But I wonder if the "big bucks" approach misses the point. Does true spiritual enlightenment result from a specific set of external stimuli administered with the regularity of train schedule? Or is it something impossible to really even quantify, much less to reproduce on demand? Are we just fooling ourselves in thinking that we can commercialize spirituality?

Consider the example of John Gill. In the beginning, he seemed no different than scores of other climbers. He focused on challenging peaks in Alaska and Yosemite, just like many of his peers. He endured the privations of altitude and cold, and he counted reaching a summit as the definition of success. And if he had continued along that path, he undoubtedly would have gained a reputation as a skilled and intrepid mountaineer. Maybe he would have even become the 34th member of the eight-thousander club.

But Gill decided to follow a radically different path. Because he was in tune with his inner voice — and because he had the courage to listen to that voice — he was able to buck climbing conventional wisdom in favor of an approach that he found more engaging, more challenging and ultimately more fulfilling. How many of us are willing to do the same?

Authentic spirituality requires us to "tune in" to the wider reality around us, to successfully align our own needs and desires to the energies of the universe. Think about it like a radio. Let's say that you really want to listen to rock, but all your friends, family and coworkers are fans of country music. Maybe you don't want to cause waves by being the outsider. Maybe you're afraid of being teased. Maybe you just want to feel like you belong. Whatever the reason, let's assume you follow the crowd and listen to country. No matter how you rationalize it, no matter how noble your intentions, the fact is that you're denying a fundamental part of your identity; you're pretending to be something you're not. Eventually the rhythms within and those without create a discordant cacophony. If you don't take steps to resolve the conflict, you'll never know the benefits — and the beauty — of true harmony.

Self-clarity is the necessary precursor to spiritual well-being. Even if you want to listen to the country music station that broadcasts at 98.7 on your FM band, but you set your dial to 99.7, all you'll hear is static. Once John Gill clearly understood what really attracted him to climbing (the technical challenges), he was able to discard what was, to him, ultimately non-essential (elevation). He was able to tune in to the frequency that was right for him and, as a result, his talent was able to find its fullest expression.

Ayurveda dates back thousands of years, as we discussed in Chapter Two. The major focus of Ayurvedic medicine is that if the forces within our bodies are kept in harmonious alignment with the surrounding environment, we can resist illness. The key word here is *balance*: balance not just of the body, but of the mind and spirit as well. A basic impulse that runs through all of us that controls overall balance, right down to the tiniest cells in our bodies. Recognizing this inherent and indivisible relationship between the spiritual and the physical, between our inner existence and our outer environment, is essential for achieving authentic alignment.

Beginning exercises

We've talked repeatedly throughout this book about the need to be patient in your journey to a healthier, happier lifestyle. Nowhere is that more true than in the area of your spiritual well-being. Is it even possible to objectively measure spiritual progress? My advice is not to try. Simply concentrate on the path itself; the rest will take care of itself.

Identify your core values

Before you can intentionally listen to your deep inner voice, you have to be able to tune into it with consistency. Here's a useful exercise for identifying the unique set of core values that inform that voice:

Step 1: Brainstorm a list of personal values. Find a quiet place and block out some time to simply write down a list of value words that come to mind. Think about the peak experiences of your life. What values were responsible for it? Conversely, reflect on times you felt intensely frustrated or upset. What values were being suppressed in those moments? Don't worry about ranking the value words you write down. Also don't worry if the some of the words on your list seem redundant — that might simply be an indicator of which values really resonate with your subconscious mind.

Step 2: Arrange your values into groups. Chances are the list you just generated is pretty large. It might contain as many as a few dozen value words, which is a bit too unwieldy for our purposes. So the next step is to look for commonalities in some of those words and group them by theme. For instance, you might group traits like "growth," "development" and "learning" together into one group.

Step 3: Identify the central theme of each group. Try to write a sentence or two describing each thematic group. Then reduce that sentence to a single word or phrase. For example, if you summarize the group we mentioned in the previous step as: "Always keep learning and growing," you might distill that down to something like "lifelong learning."

Step 4: Create a personal values mantra. Having extracted the essence of the values that matter most to you, the final step is to connect those words or phrases into a personal values mantra, a kind of spiritual mission statement that provides you with a lens though which to view the world. It doesn't have to be innovative or profound, but it does have to be authentic.

Completing this core values exercise will give you a valuable tool for aligning your actions with that inner voice — for properly tuning your inner radio dial, if you will.

Connect through writing

We talked in the previous chapter about the benefits of free-form writing in working through emotional turmoil, and that is equally true in your spiritual journey. Keeping a journal helps you reflect on the events of the day (or week) and create meaning. It can help clarify areas of confusion by allowing you to process seemingly disparate incidents and find connections. And, as we talked about before, it can be wonderfully cathartic.

It's also beneficial to have a tangible record you can refer back to from time to time to remind yourself of how you surmounted past events, no matter how dire they appeared at the time. That perspective can be tremendously useful when we're struggling to have faith or stay positive in the face of current challenges. It reinforces the notion that there is a grand design in the universe in which we all play a part.

Tune in . . . and tune out

For many of us, the duality between our inner and outer selves naturally leads to another question about spirituality: Aren't spirituality and religion different terms for the same thing?

The short answer is no.

That doesn't mean that the two are mutually incompatible. But they are fundamentally different. To paraphrase Deepak Chopra, religion is having someone else's experience; spirituality is about having your own. Religious rituals are primarily designed to create a group identity and promote conformity within that group. Religion — any religion — tends to promote a clear delineation between "us" and "them" by relying on man-made articulations of belief systems, and then judging negatively those who don't share those same beliefs.

Spirituality, on the other hand, eschews labels and definitions. It is ultimately inclusive and accepting and completely individualized. It is an inner path to be followed, not a set of external practices to be obeyed. It doesn't require regular attendance at a church, temple, synagogue or mosque. It doesn't require tithing or formal membership. It doesn't require identification with a particular group or label.

What spirituality does require is a set of core values and beliefs that are the foundational basis for everything that you do. It requires listening to that deep inner voice or intuition that comes from your higher self or truest self: your essential self. It requires allowing those purposeful feelings to become the driving force for your life, rather than trying to "force the dial" to a frequency that isn't right for you.

With all the talk about your inner radio, it probably shouldn't surprise you that actually listening to music can be very beneficial to your spiritual well-being. Commit to 10 minutes of daily listening to pieces of music that inspire you, move you or otherwise resonate with you. If you prefer, you can sing or chant instead. Several years ago, the late Wayne Dyer put together a CD called "Meditations for Manifestation" that uses a simple but very effective "ah and ohm" pattern to heighten your spiritual awareness.

Even as you use music to connect with the energy of the universe at a deeper and richer level, you might also consider opting out of negative audio and video stimuli for at least one day a week. Several studies have shown increased incidences of anxiety and depression in self-styled "news junkies." Hearing overwhelmingly negative or fear-inducing information — and let's face it, that's what our modern sensationalized media caters to — allows dissonant external energy to interrupt your internal resonance, creating spiritual disharmony.

I've been very intentional about monitoring my levels of negative video and audio input for the last 10 years. I read news in print or online, but I rarely watch any of the news channels on TV. I don't want to intentionally expose myself to the fear any more than is necessary. And by focusing instead on harmony and the potential for a better reality, I'm able to send that positive energy into the universe . . . and thereby help bring it into being. More on how that process works in the next session.

I'm as well informed as I ever was (maybe even more), but by making a conscious choice about what to interact with, I've reinforced my inner positivity. The result has been a considerable increase in clarity, energy and creativity.

Open yourself to new experiences

Your spiritual well-being depends on making yourself vulnerable to the subtle urgings of the universe. That means opening yourself up to new experiences, new connections, and new insights. Travel is obviously an invaluable mechanism for that sort of self-discovery — it takes you out of your comfort zone and opens your eyes to new sights and sounds, different customs, and unfamiliar experiences. Even a short trip can have a profound impact on your psyche.

Another equally valid — and less expensive — path to new experiences is through volunteering. The shift in perspective allows you to see your own life in a different light; perhaps it will help you re-prioritize your values, responsibilities, and ambitions. It also enables you to contribute positive energy to the universe, which should never be underestimated. In the same way, don't be afraid to let go of what no longer serves you. Re-purpose material possessions you no longer need or use so that they may go to someone who does need them. Even small acts of charity help you see and connect to the greater whole.

Why is that so? There is a set of universal laws or truths that govern everything that exists in our world. Entire books are dedicated to defining the various permutations of these universal laws, so we don't really have the time or space to go into depth here. But I do want to give you an overview so you can begin to understand the fundamental interconnectivity of all things.

Let's start with the Law of Oneness. Everything we do, believe, say or think affects not only the people around us, but in fact the whole environment around us — and through it, the greater universe. Ponder that for a moment. How does it change the intentionality with which we approach . . . well, *everything* we do?

A second law, the Law of Vibration, states that everything has its own unique vibrational frequency: sight and sound, thoughts and feelings, even physical objects. Because of the Law of Oneness, we know that each of these bandwidths is connected to the greater universe; each is intertwined with all the others.

That in turn contributes to a third law, the Law of Cause and Effect. Sometimes cause-and-effect relationships are easy to spot. A hurricane causes major flooding. You break your arm and the doctor immobilizes the joint in a cast to prevent further damage. Sometimes, however, the causality is less immediate. If, for instance, you neglect regular maintenance on your car, sooner or later it will break down. From a spiritual perspective, this is all about ensuring that you are providing yourself the spiritual care necessary to support the integration of the four areas of health.

Another law that has received a great deal of publicity in the past few years is the Law of Attraction. This law states that the energies produced by our thoughts, feelings, words and actions attract similar energies: in the simplest terms, positive energy attracts positive energy; negative energy attracts negative. Often this law is misunderstood, unfortunately: "If I think happy thoughts, only good things will happen to me." The reality is a bit more complex. Intention, consistency and alignment are absolutely key.

The final law that concerns us here is the Law of Perpetual Transmutation of Energy. The universe is always changing, always in a state of flux — a stream of consciousness is always flowing in and out of our bodies. The vibrational frequencies we talked about earlier continually interact with each other, with those at a higher vibrational state helping dissolve and transform those at lower vibrational states. In combination with the other universal laws, this means that all of us have the innate ability and power to change the conditions of our lives for the better. It's only when we are resistant to that change that things to appear to stay the same.

It's important to understand that the universal laws don't operate in isolation, but rather in concert with each other. Remember as well that they are not so much a secret to be unlocked as a lens through which to view our lives and the lives of those around us. To learn more about the universal laws, refer to the Resources section at the end of this book.

Intermediate exercises

This level is more about deepening your awareness of your own spiritual well-being than adding substantially new strategies to your repertoire. As before, remind yourself to pay attention to the journey itself rather than fretting about the destination.

Develop subtle awareness

With so many sources of stimuli competing for our attention, disrupting our focus and threatening our clarity, it's important to develop the spiritual discipline to tune out the noise and stay in tune with who we are and what we're experiencing in the moment. With practice, you can hone that skill to a remarkably high level.

One good way to begin is during your shower. Close your eyes and focus on the feel of the water drops on your head, neck, and shoulders. Listen to the sound of the water flowing down. If showering isn't your thing, try the same exercise sitting in the sun on a nice day. Focus on the feel of its warmth on your skin, or the cool whisper of the breeze. Don't label the sensations, don't think about your to-do list — just give yourself to the moment. Be completely and utterly in the moment.

The more you practice this, the better you'll become at creating and maintaining a focused awareness of the subtle nuances often ignored: your breathing, your muscles, the sensations in your body. This keeps us in tune with who we are and what we are experiencing. Some ancient martial arts masters were reputed to be able to anticipate an opponent's move by noticing almost imperceptibly tiny details: the twitch of a finger, the dilation of a pupil, the slightly altered rhythm of respiration.

When you're ready for a more challenging exercise, try this same activity in a crowded area. Drop down deep within yourself and simply observe; don't allow yourself to react. The best practice I have had was on a street in India. The sights, sounds, and smells of so many people, animals, and vehicles packed into a relatively small space can be quite literally overwhelming. Opening yourself up and allowing the waves of stimuli to wash over you and through you without disturbing your inner calm is a true test of your spiritual focus.

Deep breathing exercises

Deep breathing allows us to physiologically calm our minds and bodies, which helps us cultivate the inner stillness required for spiritual clarity. There are a number of deep breathing techniques, some of which are referenced in the Resources section at the end of the book.

That said, I would strongly recommend signing up for an Energy Codes Level 1 course (more on Energy Codes in the next section). As a certified practitioner of the Energy Codes, I often work with patients on a basic breathing exercise, Central Channel Breath. It uses the *sushumna*, an energy channel that runs from the top of the head through the crown and right down the center of the brain, throat, chest, belly and down into the pelvis.

Breathing through your nose, visualize a starting point a few inches above your head. Draw a deep, controlled breath right through that central channel deep into your belly. Exhale downward through the center channel, down into the earth. Then take another deep breath, this time visualizing it coming up from the earth into your belly; exhale straight up the central channel and out the top of your head.

Central Channel Breath utilizes a practice called Mula Bandha, a squeezing of the pelvic bowl muscles while breathing. Doing so brings our consciousness down into the body, centering us. Deep breathing like this fundamentally helps connect our spirits, minds and bodies. It's as simple as it is powerful.

Cultivate an attitude of abundance

There's no question that we live in a materialistic culture, one that advocates the continual, relentless acquisition of more . . . everything. We're constantly being bombarded with the "more is better" message — and constantly being made to feel inferior if we don't have the "right" home, vehicle, clothing, or phone. Advertisers try to foster a sense of urgency grounded in the presumption of scarcity: "Deals too good to pass up! Hurry before it's all gone!"

I've seen too many patients caught up in this rat race of acquisition, taking jobs they hated simply because the salary was too lucrative to pass up, or going into debt in a futile effort to "keep up" with everyone else by purchasing the latest and greatest, or simply trying to fill a deep spiritual void through high-dollar shopping sprees and expensive trips. In the end, nothing worked — they were some of the most profoundly unhappy people I've ever treated.

To quote the old 1980s movie *Wargames*, "The only way to win is not to play the game." Realize that our universe holds more than enough for everyone and everything. Resist the impulse to reach for more; accept that the universe, in its infinite wisdom and abundance, has given each of us exactly what we need. The secret to contentment can't be bought.

Advanced exercises

Once you're comfortable integrating spiritual awareness into your everyday life, you're ready to explore some more advanced techniques. Both of the strategies described below are best utilized with the guidance of a qualified professional.

Resonance Repatterning®

Once called holographic repatterning, Resonance Repatterning was pioneered by Chloe Faith Wordsworth, who details the technique in her book, *Quantum Change Made Easy*. It's an amazing blend of 21ˢᵗ-century science and ancient wisdom. To understand it, we have to remind ourselves of Einstein's famous $E=mc^2$ equation, which mathematically shows that matter and energy are interchangeable. Our entire reality — our bodies, our thoughts, our emotions — are simply varying frequencies of the vast interconnected universal energy field.

When those energy frequencies are in harmony, we are healthy, happy, and fulfilled. When they are less than optimal, we experience physical, mental, emotional or spiritual problems. Unfortunately, because these frequencies exist at the unconscious level of perception, we are frequently unable to identify the source of the dissonance, much less take steps to correct it.

During a Resonance Repatterning session, a practitioner first uses applied kinesiology, also called muscle strength testing. In simple terms, by evaluating the way individual muscles or groups of muscles respond to force, a trained practitioner can identify areas of dysfunction. Because those muscles are linked to various physical, mental and emotional processes, the practitioner can pretty reliably diagnose the underlying causes of dysfunction. Along with the muscle checking, the practitioner uses the Resonance Repatterning system to identify the exact unconscious beliefs that are involved with the problem.

Then the practitioner uses a variety of healing modalities (also known as Energizing Options) — including polarity therapy, acupuncture contact points, color therapy, flower remedies, nutrition and breathing patterns — to raise the frequencies in question back to their desired levels.

One practitioner of Resonance Repatterning I've personally had the privilege of working with I know is Jo Helesfay-Evans of Inner Light Holistics in the UK. Since 1998, she's been helping people find and resolve the roots of their issues and re-orient themselves on a better, happier, and healthier path. I was particularly impressed by the example of one of her patients — we'll call her Jenny — who began as a skeptic:

> I found Jo at a very low point in my life. I was experiencing extreme anxiety, panic attacks, and depression. I didn't really know what to expect from Resonance Repatterning, but decided to give it a go as I found regular counselling, for me, just brought up negative emotions but didn't really get to the root of the issue.
>
> Jo has a calming and caring manner that immediately put me at ease. It's amazing how wired up we are, but with Jo's skill she can find the problem straight away as if plucking out a past hurt that hadn't even been brought into my consciousness.
>
> Many issues that once really bothered me with relationships and jealousy faded away. My anxiety and depression decreased a lot. I also found a better work life balance and with Jo's help I began to resonate with positive changes, breaking the rut I was in and securing a job I'm far happier in.
>
> While I believe there are many contributing factors to anxiety and depression, I know Resonance Repatterning helps, especially when you have issues in relationships that are stopping you moving forward although you don't fully know why.

If you'd like to learn more about Resonance Repatterning, take a look at the Resources section at the end of this book.

The Energy Codes®

In the last chapter, we talked about the Bio Energetic Synchronization Technique (BEST) developed by Dr. M.T. Morter. Building on his work, his daughter Dr. Sue has become a world-renowned authority on bio-energetic medicine and a quantum field visionary in her own right, with over 30 years of experience as both a doctor and a master teacher of groups and individuals. Through her Energy Codes coursework, she helps individuals clear subconscious memory blockages in order to master the energetic flow in their lives and fully activate their full human potential.

Remember, the patterns of energy that inform our perceptions and ultimately determine our beliefs exist at both the conscious and subconscious level. As we've discussed previously, our subconscious beliefs are actually more potent than our conscious ones. What that means for your health is that if your subconscious mind holds energy patterns in conflict with your conscious choices, the result is stress, anxiety, and emotional turmoil.

Unlike our conscious mind, our subconscious possesses no sense of time. So when we remember — or even imagine — what our subconscious interprets as danger, it causes the body to respond as though it were actually happening in the here and now. Our heart rate increases, our muscles tighten, and our blood pressure elevates. Everything else becomes a distant priority as our body gets ready for fight or flight.

Once our subconscious perceives that the danger is gone, though, the body reverses course. Our heart rate slows, our blood pressure drops, and our muscles relax. In that state, we have access to our full range of creative, healing powers.

With Dr. Sue's guidance, Energy Codes participants explore their own awareness through practices of self-healing, meditation and inner reflection through integrative breath-work. Doing so allows them to access higher frequency energy patterns and "recode" their subconscious.

As a certified facilitator of the Energy Codes work, I've used Dr. Sue's techniques in my own practice — and my own life — with impressive results. I remember one patient in particular: a high-powered, very left-brained attorney who was by her own admission driven by demonstrable evidence and logic. She came to me complaining of persistent and severe back pain in the thoracolumbar region. I attempted to treat it using traditional chiropractic techniques, but the relief I was able to provide proved very temporary.

When I first mentioned the interrelationship between energy, emotion and physical symptoms, I thought she was going to walk out. Still, I was able to gradually introduce some Energy Codes breath-work into her treatment plan, carefully avoiding talking about the metaphysics. The results were dramatic. After eight years of nearly constant agony, within a few sessions she was almost entirely pain-free. She was sleeping well and felt more clarity and balance in her work and her personal life.

After several months, she asked me about the techniques we were using. This time, she listened without making any dismissive judgments — in fact, she wanted to know more. At my suggestion, she even began to learn some meditation techniques.

Within a year, I was helping her lead group sessions for her staff on finding inner stillness, which she believed would increase both morale and efficiency. She still ends weekly staff meetings with a short period of meditation and breath-work — quite the turnaround from the skeptic who walked into my office!

Final thoughts

It can be tempting to relegate our spiritual well-being to the proverbial back burner, to focus instead on physical pains or emotional traumas. But that approach is incomplete. Our spirituality is the foundation on which we build the life we truly want for ourselves. It is essential, not optional, to our health and happiness. And its power maximizes everything else we do in our lives. Consider the following story:

A teacher and his student were walking from one village to the next when they were surprised by a loud roar behind them. Turning quickly, they saw that a large, ferocious-looking tiger had crept within leaping range. His tail swished back and forth, and his eyes glinted dangerously.

"What should we do, master?" the student fearfully asked.

"What do you suggest, my student?" the teacher responded calmly.

"We could run!" the student exclaimed.

"We could, but the tiger is faster than we are," the teacher said. "He would surely catch us and tear us to pieces."

"There are two of us," the student offered. "We could charge the tiger!"

"We could, but the tiger is stronger than we are," the teacher responded. "He would surely overpower us and tear us to pieces."

"We could play dead!" the student said.

"We could, but the tiger is too intelligent to be fooled," the teacher said. "He would surely sense our ruse and tear us to pieces."

"Then what can we do, master?" the student asked imploringly, almost beside himself out of fear.

The teacher did not respond. Instead he closed his eyes and stood, calm and still and unafraid, as the tiger prepared to pounce on the men. The student uttered a prayer and readied himself for the next life. But when he opened his eyes, he saw that the tiger had lowered his head and tail and was walking away.

"What happened?" the bewildered young man asked.

"I cleared my mind of fear and anger and hope and simply opened my spirit to the universe," the sage answered. "In doing so, my spirit and the tiger's spirit became entwined. Sensing my peace, the tiger no longer perceived us as a threat or felt the need to express violence. And so he walked away. When the spirit is silent and calm, its peace automatically influences everything and everyone around it."

You too have the power to deeply influence everything and everyone around you. Align your core values with your inner and outer actions and you'll be amazed by the results.

Chapter Ten
Next Steps

"A journey of a thousand miles begins with a single step."

-Lao Tzu, Chinese philosopher

Life is a strange and wonderful journey sometimes, filled with surprising and unexpected second acts. Mine began growing up in the rugged terrain of western North Carolina, where we were the only Indian family within about a 70-mile radius.

We were different, and there was no way to hide it or run from it. Not that my parents were inclined to do so; they had migrated to this beautifully rural backwater from India by way of Europe and the more cosmopolitan American northeast. They wore their heritage proudly, opening the only Indian restaurant within driving distance and enthusiastically sharing their culture with patrons.

In those parts, segregation was still evident in practice, if not in law, and as a dark-skinned, dark-haired girl I definitely felt the sting of not fitting in — even though I was fortunate to develop a good support group of friends around me. Still, I felt different. I compensated in part by focusing on my studies, and by age 15 I was taking college classes, sitting surrounded by college freshmen and sophomores . . . and still not fitting in. Despite that (or maybe because I was immune to it by this time) I enjoyed the challenge and unique perspective the experience afforded me.

When I went off to university, I planned to obtain my bachelor's degree in public health nutrition. The School of Public Health was practically right across from the medical school that many of my friends attended. I soon realized that this route was not for me; it did not satisfy my inner knowledge that I wanted to be involved with much more than just the physical aspect of healing. After encouragement from my father to look into other avenues that might feel more suited to my inclinations, I decided to earn a doctorate in chiropractic. It seemed an appealing blend between the intellectual and the spiritual, a kind of perfect contradiction that my own Indian culture not only accepted, but embraced. Through it, I hoped to honor my heritage while still forging my own unique path through life. I thought I'd had it all figured out. I began to get reconnected with the wisdom of my heritage while still embracing Western practices.

That illusion was suddenly shattered a year into my practice when my mother was diagnosed with a terminal illness. I had always been close to her, but during the last year and a half of her life our relationship became even more intimate . . . and intense. Our conversations became more profound, as she imparted so much wisdom in such a short time. Watching her, I began finally really understanding the components that truly make us human: the emotional, the mental, and the physical and, perhaps most important of all, the spiritual.

I had steeled myself to be strong for her sake, but inside I felt broken. Life seemed to be on autopilot. And when she passed, her absence left an almost physical pain, a void that simply couldn't be filled.

Within a few years I lost two other close friends. It was as though I was buried beneath an avalanche of grief and uncertainty. I didn't know how to dig myself out from under the rubble — and truth be told, I didn't want to. The emotional and spiritual trauma had even begun to affect my physical health. I wasn't living; I was just marking time.

And then my second act began.

In the midst of my despair, I began to listen to my inner voice, to trust my own intuition. I picked up and moved overseas to begin an unexpected journey of healing and discovery. Until then, I hadn't realized just how many compromises I'd made to "fit in," how many times I had deferred to conventional wisdom. Now I began to understand that only by truly embracing the highs and the lows of life, only by experiencing life in all its diversity, could we expand our consciousness. I realized as never before the necessity for authentically aligning the physical, mental, emotional and spiritual aspects of our lives if we are to achieve the unique and wonderful potential contained within each of us. Only then can we discern meaning in our existence; only then can we truly live a life worth living.

As I began to follow my intuition, I began incorporating many of the practices mentioned in the preceding chapters into my own life and practice. And I found that they helped me heal, find joy, inspire others, and put into practice some of the things my mother and I had talked about during her illness. Most importantly, they allowed me — finally — to focus on being a creator of positivity rather than a victim of circumstance.

The result has been the creation of the Prasad Method. In Sanskrit, "*prasada*" has two connotations: the most common is an offering (usually food) made to the divine that is then redistributed to others as a blessing, a "gracious gift" or "enlightening." For pilgrims visiting Hindu temples, receiving this *prasada* is a major motivation.

There is, however, a second meaning. In Vedic literature, *prasada* is a mental or spiritual state achieved by "gods, sages, and other powerful beings." One of its distinguishing features is spontaneous, authentic generosity. In the Judeo-Christian tradition, it comports closely with the idea of "blessed to be a blessing to others." And the more these blessings are distributed, the more positive energy and thoughts are devoted to them, the more the Universal Power of Positive Thought works in favor of both the benefactor and the recipient.

The Prasad Method combines the techniques, philosophies and resources we've explored in the preceding chapters into a coherent, cohesive approach to total wellness. It fosters your ability to identify and resolve the underlying sources of the conflicts — both internal and external — that are sabotaging your life, career and relationships. It allows you to bring your physical, mental, emotional and spiritual selves into authentic and sustainable alignment in order to be happier, healthier, more energetic and more creative.

To learn more about the Prasad Method, and how it can help you achieve the life you've given up hope of having, please take a few minutes and visit www.theprasadmethod.com.

Sustaining your health journey

Like life itself, achieving aligned health is a journey without a destination. It's not a quick fix, or even a "to do" item to be checked off your list. The techniques profiled throughout this book are designed to offer you adaptable, sustainable, and lifelong tools.

How do you know if it's working? Honestly, the way that you feel is the number one indicator. Are you feeling more relaxed than previously? Are you enjoying yourself? Do you find yourself less drained and more energized at the end of the day? If so, that's a great sign of progress.

Focus on small steps. Take your time. Be patient with yourself, especially if and when progress doesn't happen as fast as you would like. Don't beat yourself up. Good things *will* happen if you give them sufficient time and space. Above all, practice listening to your own internal guidance system. Trust your inner wisdom to tell you what is right for you in any given moment.

As we've talked about before, there's tremendous value in daily journaling as a means of recording your journey and tracking your progress. Don't be afraid to dream big, to set ambitious health goals. But be sure to mark and celebrate the smaller milestones along the way. Again, the real focus here is not reaching a specific goal; it's about the journey itself, about achieving the full expression of your truest, healthiest self.

A few years ago, I had a patient who seemed trapped in a destructive cycle. For a few months, he would make progress towards a healthier lifestyle: eating better, exercising more, being more deliberate about his spiritual practices. And then he'd have a setback, which would send him into a spiral of self-recrimination and guilt.

After several rounds of this yo-yoing, I asked him about his favorite dessert. He told me it was dark chocolate. "Great!" I told him. "The next time you meet a goal, rather than second-guess yourself or obsess about how much more there is to do, I want to you celebrate it with a decadent dark chocolate treat."

A few months later, he showed up with a beautifully wrapped gift box containing — you guessed it — some gourmet dark chocolates and a bouquet of tulips. He told me that he thought my advice was silly at first, but he had decided to give it a chance. He was amazed at its effectiveness; it had helped him be more conscious about loving himself, appreciating his body and recognizing how far he'd come on his health journey. I'd encourage you to follow his example — don't sweat the small stuff, celebrate it!

Finding a health care provider team

No matter how conscientiously you follow the guidelines laid out in this book, it's important to find a health care provider you trust. The journey to aligned health is not one you should undertake alone; some of the treatments can only be administered by a trained or certified professional, and other underlying health issues may require medication or more active monitoring.

Finding the right health care provider can be a challenging, often frustrating experience. So often bureaucratic barriers and insurance-related obstacles obscure the process of finding the provider who is the best fit for your individual needs. Don't settle! The time and effort you spend up front is an investment well worth making.

As you consider which providers are the best people to guide and advise you on your journey, here are some questions you can use to help inform the process. Remember, though, the very first step is to establish your own beliefs about the nature of health and wellness. Be sure to articulate that philosophy as you interact with prospective providers.

- Does the doctor or health care provider share your personal philosophy of health?

- Does the health care provider seem more interested getting to the root of health dysfunction, or in simply providing quick relief from painful symptoms?

- How often does the health care provider prescribe or recommend pharmaceuticals? Are they intended primarily for short-term relief or long-term use?

- Can you schedule a get-to-know-you appointment before you decide on whether or not this health care provider is a good fit for you?

- Is the health care provider open to alternative care methods or Eastern philosophies of healing? What's their level of experience with these healing modalities?

- Is the health care provider compassionate?

- Are they willing to collaborate with other providers on your health care team, or do they prefer to work solo?

- How much time do you want your health care provider to spend with you during each visit? Do you want to get in and get out as quickly as possible, or do you prefer a more casual style?

- Can you speak to the health care provider honestly and openly?

- Will this health care provider just accept things or will they try to help you find the answers or help out there?

It is vitally important that you trust the people to whom you are entrusting your health. You should feel safe and comfortable in their care; you should feel valued and listened to. If you don't, it can hinder your ability to truly heal. I recommend that you take the time to interview all prospective health care providers. Be up front and clear about your preferences and expectations in a health care partner — doing so on the front end will save you time and trouble later on.

Next steps

The noted French philosopher Pierre Teilhard de Chardin once remarked, "We are not human beings having a spiritual experience. We are spiritual beings having a human experience." Being really, truly healthy means accepting that our well-being is more than a set of numbers on a blood test or a scale. Health is so much more than meets the eye; it really is the foundation of who we are. It requires an authentic alignment of our physical, mental, emotional and spiritual selves — a holistic and honest approach that will transform how you see yourself and how you see the world around you.

I have been fortunate to witness that type of change, both in my own life and in the lives of my patients and clients, and I can attest to the value of making the changes discussed in the pages of this book. Start small, start slow — but start now! Don't delay! You, and only you, have the power to transform your life with passion, dedication and desire. You can change your path; you can create a richer, more fulfilling journey. I've seen it. I've done it.

I hope you'll consider me both a resource and a cheerleader on that journey to a healthier, happier, more authentically aligned life. I encourage you to take a few moments to visit my websites, www.ashaprasad.com or www.theprasadmethod.com, and explore some of the options for further information and additional resources, as well as share your own successes.

In the meantime, let me leave you with one of my favorite quotes from the great psychologist Carl Jung — and a great perspective to help inform your journey: "The privilege of a lifetime is to become who you truly are."

Resources

Chapter 1
The Biology of Belief: Unleashing the Power of Consciousness, Matter, and Miracles, by Bruce Lipton (Hay House, 2008)

Take the Lead (PG-13, 2006)

Chapter 2
Ayurveda: The Divine Science of Life, by Todd Caldecott (Mosby, 2006)

The Complete Book of Ayurvedic Home Remedies, by Vasant Lad (Harmony, 1999)

The Gift of Pain: Why We Hurt and What We Can Do About It, by Paul Brand and Philip Yancey (Zondervan, 1997)

Chapter 3
You Can Heal Your Life, by Louise Hay (Hay House, 1984) (A 2007 movie with the same title is also recommended.)

Steve Jobs, by Walter Isaacson (Simon & Schuster, 2015)

Chapter 6
Mornings on Horseback: The Story of an Extraordinary Family, a Vanished Way of Life and the Unique Child Who Became Theodore Roosevelt, by David McCullough (Simon & Schuster, 1982)

Autobiography of a Yogi, by Paramahansa Yogananda (Self-Realization Fellowship, 1998)

Loving Yourself to Great Health: Thoughts and Food—the Ultimate Diet, by Louise Hay, Ahlea Khadro, and Heather Dane (Hay House, 2015)

All is Well: Heal Your Body with Medicine, Affirmations and Intuition, by Louise Hay and Mona Lisa Schulz (Hay House, 2014)

www.yogabasics.com/practice/yoga-for-beginners/

www.qigonginstitute.org

www.pranarom.com

Dr. Sue Morter's video on the Tibetan Rites (https://vimeo.com/120608792)

Chapter 7

Angels of Abundance: Heaven's 11 Messages to Help You Manifest Support, Supply, and Every Form of Abundance, by Doreen Virtue and Grant Virtue (Hay House, 2014)

Chakra Cleaning, by Doreen Virtue (Hay House, 1998)

www.stillnessproject.com

The Complete Guide to Vision Boards, by Christine Kane (http://christinekane.com/yours-for-free-the-complete-guide-to-vision-boards-and-other-gifts-too/)

Chapter 8

www.morter.com (BEST techniques)

The Pursuit of Happyness (PG-13, 2006)

Chapter 9

www.drsuemorter.com (Energy Codes)
www.innerlightholistics.com (Resonance Repatterning)
www.life-spotter.com (Resonance Repatterning)
www.mindvalley.com/products/omharmonics

Meditations for Manifesting: Morning and Evening Meditations to Literally Create Your Heart's Desire (audiobook), by Wayne Dyer (Hay House, 2004)

The Shift (PG, 2009)

General Resources

Peaceful Warrior (PG-13, 2013)

3 Idiots (PG-13, 2011)

The Four Agreements: A Practical Guide to Personal Freedom, by Don Miguel Ruiz (Amber-Allen Publishing, 1997)

The Alchemist, by Paulo Coelho (HarperOne, 2014)

The Five People You Meet in Heaven, by Mitch Albom (Hyperion, 2006)

Oh, The Places You'll Go! by Dr. Seuss (Random House, 1990)

The Power of Now: A Guide to Spiritual Enlightenment, by Ekhart Tolle (Namaste Publishing, 2004)

Tao Te Ching: An Illustrated Journey, by Lao Tzu and Stephen Mitchell (Frances Lincoln, 2009)

Universal Laws: 18 Powerful Laws & The Secret Behind Manifesting Your Desires, by Jennifer O'Neil (CreateSpace Independent Publishing, 2013)

Cosmic and Universal Laws: Subtitle Infinite Laws for a Happy and Prosperous Life, by Margo Kirtikar (Trafford Publishing, 2008)

www.hayhouse.com

www.ted.com/talks

About the Author

Asha M. Prasad attained her Bachelor of Science in Public Health from the University of North Carolina-Chapel Hill and earned her Doctorate of Chiropractic from Life Chiropractic University in Marietta, Georgia. She is also a certified practitioner of B.E.S.T. (Bioenergetics Synchronization Technique) and an Advanced Certified Facilitator of the Energy Codes® and has been in private practice in the United States and Europe.

In addition to her work with patients, Dr. Asha is also a mentor and consultant, helping both individuals and organizations align personal and professional goals, increase productivity, improve customer relationships, and boost overall vitality and creativity.

Visit **www.theprasadmethod.com** or connect with Dr. Asha on Facebook to learn more about The Prasad Method™ and how it can improve the quality of your life and career.

Lightning Source UK Ltd.
Milton Keynes UK
UKHW020746160921
390677UK00009B/298